What Else Can I Do on the Internet?

Nicholl McGuire

Nicholl McGuire Media
United States of America

What Else Can I Do on the Internet?

Published by Nicholl McGuire Media

ISBN 978-1505637625

Table of Contents

Introduction

Do more while you are seated at your computer other than visit the same old sites! Break those daily routines that make you feel tired before you even get started performing your important computer tasks. In this book, you will find many great activities to do as well as an abundance of useful ways to get the most out of your Internet experiences. Now be advised, this guide is an idea generator. It provides tips on how to find useful, entertaining and interesting websites that will help you do things like: create, communicate, build, promote, and teach others online. You just might find yourself on the Internet doing new and exciting things for hours! The key is to take what you already do online and build upon that knowledge by discovering how you can do more to enhance your Internet experiences.

When I first began my World Wide Web (www) experience back during the winter of 1993, I was so excited. I was about to turn what little computer knowledge I had into something big for me. Back then, I had made my first new multi-media desktop computer purchase. It was almost $1500 which was a bit over-priced at the time. I went into a local department store to buy it against the advice of someone who was quite familiar with making purchases online. I had yet to wrap my head around buying stuff via computer. I was still thinking like so many at the time, "What if someone steals my credit card info...What if the item doesn't make it to my door? What if it breaks?" So I shelled out more money because I wasn't quite ready to start buying stuff off the Internet. Little did I know at the time, I needed to build my confidence in something that was actually helping many more people than hurting them.

Around the same time I made my computer purchase, I received an America Online disk in the mail -- I was all-too-ready to use it. This disk was a big deal back in the 1990's because it gave you access to the web. These disks were sent everywhere. I didn't know anyone who didn't get the America Online software in their snail mail. For less than $10 a month, you could surf, play games, and do other fun stuff online. This was yet another thing that was going to boost my entertainment time. Besides playing computer games like Solitaire and using word processing and desktop publishing software, I was going to have a bit of fun going online. I had grown up during the stone age of big, bulky computer world back when there were no windows and all you had was a green cursor flashing at you waiting for you to type some DOS code to make it do something. So I didn't always have patience and I found that what some companies advertised as a fast Internet connection really wasn't to me.

Once I got started using my computer, I couldn't stop talking with relatives and friends about how much I could do on it. Some were in the process of upgrading from their archaic systems to computers with media capabilities too. I recall the first time I listened to music on my computer through four speakers, watched video, chatted live via the web, sent an email, and searched for information--it was overwhelming! I couldn't believe the vast amount of things I could accomplish in an hour. Nowadays you can do much in mere seconds!

But like with all good things, there are sure to be some issues right around the corner. There were those modem issues. Your grandparents or great grandparents might remember having to listen to their devices to ensure they had properly connected with the server in order to get online. So they waited for the series of beeps to sound. Hopefully all went well or else they had to reboot. The process could take anywhere from five minutes to an hour plus depending on one's connection speed, how many people were logging on, and what company provided the service. Then there were those images that seemed to take forever to pop up on computer screens once a user was logged onto the World Wide Web. We hated to click on a site with many graphics. I recall resenting the numerous ads back then. Anyway, I was turned off with so many sites that wanted me to buy this or that and even to date I don't like the banner ads and rarely click on them.

Back in the 90's, sometimes those ads got in the way of the information people were trying to read and there were those that just didn't go away easily. No little "x" sign to close, so one would sweep it away or click the screen in the foreground to continue reading. If there were too many ads in the background, the individual's computer would crash causing him or her to have to reboot. Pop-ups here and there--what a mess back then! Probably still is if one is too cheap to buy malware removal tools and virus software. So far, notice how I share with you a bit about my computer background experience. With each challenge I was faced with, I was growing in knowledge. I stayed motivated and confident in my abilities. As you learn more things in this book, you will need to be dedicated to each task until you can master them.

As the Internet got older and our society moved into the 2000s, the marketers got cleverer when it came to filling our email inboxes with a bunch of junk. Some people I knew were getting scammed and a few times I found something on my computer from clicking on what I thought were legitimate emails. Trying to figure out what was virus free was sometimes a challenge, because the scammers were getting slicker and improvements were constantly being made, like to day, on virus software. In time, it was a blessing to see the spam inboxes show up to filter the junk, control pop ups, remove cookies, unsubscribe from mailing lists, and sweep and block unwanted mail. To date, maintaining control over one's mail is still an ongoing issue. When a problem like this arises, this is where the advanced Internet user will look to find tools, new developments and more that will help him or her solve this issue. You will soon discover in this guide that when there is a new thought presented to you, you will want to do more things to build upon what you already know. This will happen quite often as you read, and you will find yourself stopping many times to look something up on the Internet.

In the past, I didn't quite connect my offline problems with online solutions right away. There were times that I would still think about going to the library, calling someone, or looking at one of my old books on a shelf to get answers. I had to keep reminding myself, "Just go on the web..." I don't quite remember when I went from saying web to the Internet, but as times change so do we. This might be something that some of you readers still do. You forget about the Internet or talk yourself out of going online in the hopes that you can solve a problem without need of it. Then before long, minutes or hours have gone by and you end up going online anyway.

As I became more experienced using the computer and Internet, I was often surprised by the new activities that seemed to pop up over night. During my early Internet experiences, online banking was one of the best features to make life so much simpler when it came to paying bills. We online bill payers learned to set and forget. However, if one wasn't too careful and your paycheck was not consistent, you just might overdraft or some weird thing once in awhile would occur where one needed to check with his or her bank. Despite the hiccups, even now, I still love the convenience and not having to worry if my check made it to a company or individual while wondering when he or she plans to cash it (sigh).

When photo uploading and downloading came along, I enjoyed this so much too. I could share photos with my social networks that they hadn't seen in years. Some viewers cried with happiness while others complained about the way they looked in the images. I was so happy to be able to download photos from online photo albums and social networking sites that I would have never been able to get had I visited relatives' homes. When I made my first photo printer purchase I was ecstatic, because I could print out what I wanted when I wanted and send to whomever. That is until I started noticing how quickly the cost of buying ink cartridges added up. Prices have come down somewhat, depending on your printer, but I don't print like I used to. For many photos, it is just better to select your photos, upload online and then go to the local photo development center in your neighborhood to pick up. You will find in this guide many things you can do creatively.

When blogging came on the scene, I was in my heaven. Being a writer that participated in contests, published newsletters, and wrote diary entries, this was just the outlet I needed. I also liked some interesting features like being able to type on a black screen rather than a white one online. I soon discovered that I could play free music online while I wrote or listened to audio books without having to work my computer's CD drive. Funny, CDs are a thing of the past as I write. They are like audio tapes, 8 tracks, vinyl records, as well as other recording products, although the items are dated and not considered the best and the greatest. But anyone who likes to save money doesn't want to keep buying media over and over again, so you tend to keep your players around.

Those days of renting VHS and DVD movies at the local Blockbuster had stopped for all of us previous members when we started choosing to watch movies online rather than leave home during the mid-2000s. Documentaries were readily available on video sharing websites as well. I couldn't imagine having to stand in line ever again to rent a movie (that is if I am at a theater or library).

I realized the benefits of using the Internet mentally, physically and spiritually more so when I started having children. The Internet was my escape from boredom at home, fussy babies who would eventually fall asleep, and a place to go to ease my mind when I needed to know something. For instance, I couldn't always get out to the doctor and oftentimes there wasn't anything so bad occurring with me or my children that required a doctor's visit, so I can't tell you how much money I saved just looking up symptoms on WebMd and other similar sites.

When I discovered there were videos and pictures I could view online related to symptoms, I felt so relieved. In addition, when the children needed certain items, I didn't hesitate to look online for a coupon, once again saving more money. Then I found sites that could help with reducing medical expenses and save on prescription costs. I also learned about alternatives to prescription medicines that worked just as good depending on the health ailment. Not all old school remedies were outdated and ineffective and I learned this after spending time reading many comments about different products in forums and websites where products were being advertising. So from this example, you can see how one task started a chain reaction to other tasks I could perform on the Internet. This is what you will find throughout this guide.

The Internet was also a life saver when I worked on certain tasks on jobs. I could simply look up whatever I needed or collaborate with others online. If I didn't know something and even still to date, I learn about it and work with the available programs right online.

When I started learning to drive, I used the Internet to take quizzes and watched videos to help understand road rules. I found useful information about what cars were considered the safest to drive, cost less money to insure, and had the best features for me. Some sites offered many images and videos to help with making a choice. I chatted online with sales representatives who were eager to meet with me.

My Internet experiences I shared with you was just a small fraction of the many things I have done and still do online, but the book you are about to read will get into some more ways to best use the Internet and get the most out of each task you create for yourself and it all starts with good research! Tips are also presented in this guide.

When seated in front of your computer, browsing from one site to the next, you might sometimes feel like you are missing out on something, because you are stuck in routines, and you are. Every time you sit in front of your computer screen, you need to have some idea what you want to learn about, how long you are going to be online finding out about it, but also you have to have the discipline to know when to leave too.

Don't overlook any opportunity online or off that might make your life a little less stressful. I sincerely hope this book helps you get even more out of your Internet experiences, so let's get started!

1 Communications

Lots of talking is done on the Internet. But the types of tools and websites to use to talk are what make the communication experience fun or dull. Choosing how you want to primarily communicate with others is essential, because once you give them an email address, online phone number, a social media name or something else, you are telling individuals, "This is my preference," so from that point on most people are going to reach out to you that way first. Gone are those days where most people only communicate via phone. They are also asking, "How else can I get a hold of you?"

Chat Rooms

A great place to air out your thoughts and meet new people are in chat rooms. You can go in these rooms as an observer just scrolling down conversation after conversation on a particular subject. Let's say there was something you thought might be a scam. Visit a chat room to see what people are saying about it. What if you saw something on TV and wondered whether you should bother buying it, search for online chat rooms and then include whatever it is you had in mind to buy. You will see live chats occurring about a wide variety of subjects.

Chat rooms are also used in plenty of ways around the Internet. You might find live chat connected with a website's front page. Sometimes a pop up window or icon will suddenly show up if you linger too long on a site, "May I help you…Do you need any help?" Respond to the live chat with your question. On banking sites, you have a choice to use live chat for your customer service concern rather than using the phone and having to hold for a long time. There are chat room apps that make it easy to chat with friends using your mobile device.

Create Your Own Chat Room or Join an Existing One

Search your topic and include keyword "chat room" or "chat rooms". When joining a chat room, you will need to select a user name. You can get ideas for user names simply by searching "user name ideas." When conversing online, most websites have chat room etiquette. The rules are usually posted somewhere on the site and some will not permit you to use a room until you have read their terms. Most people don't bother reading the rules for chat rooms before joining, but you might want to. Each chat room has a different set of rules. While one might not mind a little promotion of your webpage or business, another might suspend or ban you if you should do it.

Here are a few tips you might want to consider when visiting a chat room according to Wikihow, a how-to website. "Introduce yourself to everyone in the room…" just like you would if you were to visit a friend's home with many guests, you do the same when in a chat room. "State your question clearly and your reason for arriving." The site also advises the following: be civil to others, give the room a chance to answer you, don't spam or flood the room with repeated statements, questions, etc., avoid using colors, typing in all caps and asking A/S/L which is someone's age, sex, and location. Lastly, Wikihow mentions, if you want to open an Instant message window with someone you don't know, ask first.

Chat Lines

There are still chat lines from days past still around. You can call someone via your computer or mobile device and begin a discussion right away. Afterward set up a blind date or you can check out the person via the Internet before you bother to go out with them. You can ask them to send you a video privately using a site like YouTube or record a video using their mobile device.

Chatting for Amusement

Check out online chat rooms that are available based on your special interests or just for the sake of fun. Examples of chat rooms for various types of people include: seniors, lonely people, teens, kids, moms, writers, depressed, singles, and women. Chat rooms for fun include: international chat, social groups, kids chat, travel, sports, music, shopping, and more.

Live Chat Dating

For those who online date, "live chat" is an easy way to get to know someone rather than wasting gas meeting them somewhere only to find out you have little or no common interests. Singles take advantage of this feature on many dating websites. They simply click a button or link on a dating profile after joining a site. Then they begin chatting with members they are interested in dating on and offline. If you prefer to chat with someone you can see, there are dating sites that have video chat available. One site I found lets visitors chat with United States military singles, another Hispanic singles, Asian Singles, and people in your local community, as well as many more ethnicities. Simply put in the type of people you would enjoy talking to and begin to browse dating websites that provide different ways to communicate. See more about dating in Chapter 11.

Business Chat

If you have an existing business, you might want to find ways to incorporate live texting or chatting. It is so convenient and easy to use and keeps your work setting noise down. Instead of listening to many employees talking on phones all at the same time; instead, they could be sending messages to customers online. Chapter 3 provides more detail about business related tasks.

Forums

A forum is an online public meeting place for you to exchange ideas, comment on the latest happenings and meet new friends. These come in handy when you want to learn more about something, vent about an experience, organize something, introduce something new, share knowledge etc. Looking at past discussion boards are quite helpful especially if you have a problem similar to others and wonder how they solved their issues.

One might be having a hard time making friends offline or is lonely, searching a forum for referrals to useful websites can help. If you need additional information about a community, have a personal concern or assistance from locals in or around the area where you are located, seek out community forums in your area. Enjoy the ease of having a conversation about all sorts of subject matter from the comfort of one's home, but don't use your real name. You might not want someone to easily identify you especially if it is a personal matter you are bringing up in a forum.

Find group discussions based on your interest. If you enjoy gardening, landscaping, sewing, reading the Holy Bible, designing clothes, creating hairstyles, or painting, chances are there is a chat room of like-minded people.

Snail Mail

According to Wikipedia.org, "Snail mail and smail (from snail + mail)—named after the snail with its slow speed —refers to letters and missives carried by conventional postal delivery services." These days we live in a fast-paced society that often wants every-thing now. Snail mail is typically the last option most will use when getting documents to one another. However, when you are in need of special package pick up or drop off services, need to know latest prices to ship, need mail receipts, stamps sent to you, and more, you will want to stop by the United States Postal Service (USPS) website or other mail delivery service websites in your local area. You can do this simply by searching "mail delivery services" and include your hometown.

Shipping Online (UPS, USPS)

When ordering items prices vary depending on how fast you need your items. Be sure when you shop online you view options before sending over your payment. Sometimes there are free shipping promotions. Search the name of the company or check the website for free shipping codes. These tend to increase during holiday seasons. Some websites will specifically list companies that are promoting free shipping for that day, so be on the look out for your favorite store being featured. Also, don't forget to take advantage of "Ebates," those online rebates you receive when you shop.

Shipping calculators, rates and even employment opportunities are on postal and parcel delivery websites. Online sellers will choose a delivery service to ship products to customers and then provide proof that the package has been shipped. Tracking information is extremely helpful when you need to know your package location.

Once you received your email receipt of your purchase, most likely tracking information was listed. You can either click on the tracking information within the email (if it is a clickable link) or you can copy and paste tracking and then place it in a box provided on the delivery service's website. Although letter writing via snail mail isn't as popular as it once was, there are still useful and fun things you can do with your mail. Below are some ideas:

1. Remove your name off of all junk mail lists. There are services you can register for online.

2. Obtain a snail mail pen pal for your children.

3. Utilize an anonymous snail mail service.

4. Create personalized letters and have them delivered to family and friends.

5. Design customized shipment labels, envelopes, invoices and more.

6. Have your face or someone you know placed on a stamp.

7. Check out various snail mail games, sweepstakes and newsletters.

Social Networking

Being able to socialize with relatives, friends, co-workers and others based on your interests via the Internet is here to stay. Dictionary.com defines social networking as "the development of social and professional contacts; the sharing of information and services among people with a common interest." So if you prefer to update everyone in your network with your latest life events rather than call them, then this is the way to go. You can do this by performing a keyword search "social networking websites" now if you want a more detailed search add the kind of groups that might interest you. There is something for everyone online. Start with the "top social networking sites." Feel free to connect with me via my Facebook business page here.

When joining a site, be sure to put information in your profile that you only feel comfortable with and check privacy settings. Each site has a purpose, so know in advance why you are joining. For instance, Facebook is chocked with many distasteful photos and those images can pop up anywhere if you don't check settings. Be mindful of photos you upload and other personal things, because you never know when an employer or someone else important in your life might stop by. You can check for Facebook alternatives if you prefer to be more discreet. Be sure to change your name.

When I started registering with social networking sites back in 2005, I wanted the most popular ones at the time. I enjoyed chatting in the forums, but I wanted a page that people could visit to see referral links I had posted of advertisers, check out my personal work, and connect with old friends. In time, I found additional ones through the search engines and selected those based not only on activity, but ease of use. You can check out my page on Twitter @nichollmcguire.

People mainly upload photos to their social media pages and do other things like: update one another on the latest happenings in their lives, reconnect with old friends, view online picture albums, share other websites, learn about one another's interests, get leads to things like jobs, store bargains, and places to live if one is relocating.

When used for good intentions, social networking is a wonderful way to stay connected to the people online you care about. Yet, sometimes it can get out of hand especially if you are not careful who you allow in your network.

Take the time to check out the various social media outlets simply by searching "social media websites" or "social networking" then include your interest. Each site will ask you to register, upload a photo (which it doesn't have to be your face—it could be a pet, an abstract an image, or a picture of a car) and you will be required to include your birth date (which is not a requirement that it be displayed,) and an email address.

Nowadays you don't have to bother creating a personal page if you don't want to; there are people willing to do it for you for any purpose. You can search on Fiverr, a site or a similar website that permits sellers to offer you this service and other ones.   Once your page is completed by a worker, you can change your password so that the one who created it can't go back in and change some things. Then you just interact with those in your network whenever you want.

Email

Electronic mail allows you to send messages to someone over an Internet server rather than through snail mail. Some people don't think email is important. They communicate online and don't bother to offer their email address. In days past you use to exchange phone numbers, but nowadays email is still hanging on, but if one has a smart phone, he or she is more likely to send a text for short messages.

Email is still a great service especially when you don't want to give out your phone number and you have lengthy attachments to send. Now if you should find that you can't send a large attachment via the normal way then you send email. You will need to pay attention to alternatives to send it. When you attempted to send the file, you most likely received an option about sending it through a different drive online that has a larger capacity. Utilize this service. If you don't see any alternative options pop up, you can save the file to an online storage drive and share a link with your recipient so that he or she can open the file.

There are some limitations depending on what service you go with and there might be a fee depending on the size of the files. For instance, Google has an online drive where you can permit certain people to access your documents through that system. There is ample space to save videos, documents and anything else you have. Learn more about "online drives" and also "backup online storage." Backup storage is great if you have numerous photos and other items that you want to keep safe and stored in an additional place just in case your items are ever lost offline.

Remind yourself to provide your email address when communicating with others. So many people still forget to share email or are very protective about their address like it is a phone number. You don't have to provide your main personal email address or your company one. Create one specifically for socializing. Oftentimes, people set up one email for purchases, another for family and friends, and they might even have another email for business. Tell a person the best way to get in contact with you. Those that are computer users wouldn't be offended in the least if you just give out your email. They too might prefer contact via email then be disrupted by a phone ring. Always ask new contacts how they prefer to be reached: text, email, phone, etc.

There are many websites offering free email service. Simply type "free email" in your search engine. As of this writing, Hotmail, Yahoo and Google's Gmail are the most popular. You can also send a text to a cell phone from the Internet. To learn more, type in "send text online" in your search engine browser.

The first thing you will want to do is check the features that are offered to you. Most often an email provider creates a tour for you to learn about the company's new features. If not, conduct a search within the box located on the company's site, next add what you would like to do. For instance, I might want to include a photo I took with my camera phone and send it to a friend. (Learn more about doing cool things with images in the Creativity chapter of this book). I would include the email address in the box provided and then look for something called "attachments" or check for some kind of icon that would allow me to attach a photo to my email.

You may want to change the theme of your email, font or do some other unique stuff. Explore your email features simply by clicking all the tabs and icons. Find out what each does prior to being tested one day by someone with a friendly request like, "Could you send me an email please and attach what you have?"

Phone

You can make a call via the Internet. This comes in handy when you live at a location where the phone line no longer works or was never installed in a room. To date, Skype is popular, but there are many others. Following are more ways to communicate using the web. If you would like to research any one of these services, be sure you put the headers of each paragraph in the search engine to learn more.

Text via computer or phone - SMS Messages

You can send a text message (SMS) from your computer (email account) to a phone. Search for free text messages from your PC or use previous information as keyword phrases. You can also send a text from your cell phone to your email. Get the person's email, and then include it in your contacts. When you want to send an image, photo, text, etc. select the email option and simply hit send.

Live messages/messenger

The live message service is available on the Internet. You can use this instead of sending an email to someone if you need a quick response back. With this option, it gives you the ability to talk or type with a person in real time--that is if they are logged on. Many people have downloaded social networking apps on to their phones and will text live via the live message service provided. Text instant messaging and video conversations is what most people like to do rather than wait to receive an email or snail mail. Search for "live messages" or "send instant messages" to see what is available to date. Some employers like using this service when they are unable to work on site. They will rely heavily on live services to see that a worker is at his or her desk performing tasks.

Conference Calls

Video conferences or conference calls for listening are often used with businesses. You can learn how to set up a conference call, find out which providers are affordable, and invite others to join in on your meetings. A couple pet peeves about using this service is background noise and not being able to get on a call. There are features that will mute background noise, make additional lines available, etc. Search for online conference call web-sites and software to learn more.

Webinars

A webinar is a web-based seminar. Instead of people gather-ing in a board room, they sit in front of their computer screens watching a presentation via the Internet while chatting live from anywhere around the world. Companies typically use webinars to present lectures, workshops, seminars, and more online. Although they are not done in-person, they save businesses thousands. You can learn more about how to do things like conduct one, listen to different types or by signing up for training courses that use webinars. For example, if you wanted to know more about how to market a retail store, you could search for a series of webinars about the subject.

Things you might want to find out more about:
- Phone Number Search or Reverse Calling
- Block phone calls offline, online
- How to forward calls from a landline to computer
- How to send calls from computer to cell phone
- How to forward calls from a cell phone to a landline

Check to see if there are additional costs to use these features before you sign up for service.

2 Creativity

Your offline images need a home online. Your patchwork creations, clothing designs, building blue prints, kid's artwork, or some
other skill might be in demand by an online company. If you
haven't started a place of your own online to display your work,
you may want to build a site or get someone to do it for you.

Art
Whether you go to a museum offline or create your own artwork online, there are so many ways to communicate one's muse.
Take for instance the many artists who surf the Internet for their
next inspiration, others who upload their work for sell, and those
who enjoy sharing their thoughts with the world. If you enjoy
creating work that moves people, then you might want to take your
work to the next level.

Be open to the possibility of enhancing your craft. There are
many classes online that will help you do more with your work.
Rather than search for general terms related to your interest, be
more specific and include names of some people you admire who
do what you do.

Find new sites that allow you to do a number of fun things
online. One day I came across an entertaining site for those who
enjoy doing creative things with faces. The downloadable link was
free and before long I discovered I could do so much with my
existing photos. I have also viewed sites where I can create my
own stories using animated figures or others someone else has
drawn.

On your computer, you most likely have a software program called, "Paint." This program allows you to do a variety of things. You can freely draw, upload photos, artwork and other images and add your creations to them. Take a moment to look at what you already have on your computer and start tapping into your creative genius.

Check out the latest trends in your art genre. After surfing around the net, I noticed an offer to upload some images for sell. Although the requirements were quite specific, I learned at the time what people really wanted to see and kept that in mind before I submitted anything.

Many times I have stumbled on sites that display many unique things people do with their art. Some will offer how-to tutorials while others will take you on a shopping experience to help you obtain needed supplies. I have viewed some artists take the most mundane things and turn them into masterpieces right before my eyes.

If you are curious about what more you can do with your talent, I suggest visiting websites that have the latest books, audio, and visuals. Also, check out forums, online clubs, and other places that you can connect with individuals like yourself. I joined many sites over the years that catered specifically to writers. I also registered with websites that paid me to write, share recordings and photos. To date, I still enjoy watching the latest videos on how to paint specific things to add in my acrylic paintings. Over the years, I have also encouraged my children to watch online videos to help them play musical instruments; learn to draw, complete school work, practice for sports, fix computer issues, and more.

Blogs

The "blog" word didn't exist in anyone's vocabulary many years ago, but now it seems that's all you hear will people talk about their work or someone else's online. "She has a blog…Did you read what he put on his blog? I enjoy blogging…I am a blogger."

Blogging is simply online journal writing, but it has since expanded into many different things from a place to display artwork to a showcase for videos. People create mini-websites that include things like their thoughts about current events, family, products, and many other things useful and not. They upload photos and allow others to comment. Some will include advertising where they will receive a portion of the proceeds whenever someone clicks on an ad or places an order.

If you are the type that keeps a diary, you just might want to make a little money off your diary entries. Create a blog and then include advertising on your blog. Every time someone reads your material, they will notice an ad on your site and may click on it. You can learn more about blogging in numerous ways. If you like watching videos, search for "how to blog videos." If you prefer to read more about blogging, then type "How to create blog" and if you simply want to look at other people's blogs then go to one of the best and easiest sites to date used by bloggers, Blogger. Also, you can check out Wordpress. For tools to enhance your blog, in addition to the ones provided on Blogger or Wordpress, just keyword search: Blogger tools or Wordpress tools. Another suggested keyword is "add ons."

Vlogs

People enjoy creating videos of themselves and the environments they visit. A vlog which is a video log or journal tells of a person's life, thoughts, and dreams. If you are not good at writing you might consider a vlog. One popular video sharing place is YouTube, but also check for others by using the keywords: "YouTube alternatives" (Read more about video in this chapter).

So are blogs or vlogs essential? Well it all depends on who you ask. If you have a lot on your mind and want to vent, then a personal blog about your daily activities dealing with XYZ issue/problem/concept/person/place/thing might be useful to you and possibly others. If you feel that you need to communicate with people via video about your highs and lows or teach others, then a vlog might be helpful to you. People use blogs and vlogs for therapeutic purposes, share information with relatives and friends, sell items, communicate thoughts, or enlighten the public on any number of topics.

Here are just some ways blogs and vlogs are used on the Internet.

Blog Uses

•   Product research and commentary with coupon codes included.
•   Newsworthy events with personal thoughts.
•   New baby announcements and bay milestones.
•   Family updates.
•   Inform the public on scams.
•   Celebrity news you wouldn't see or hear about on the news.
•   Spiritual issues, biblical stories, personal experiences, and words of encouragement not often heard in main-stream churches.

Vlog Uses
- Travel journeys with personal commentary/experiences.
- Medical surgeries.
- Dating experiences.
- Shopping and preparation for new product purchases.
- Story-telling about work.
- Artwork created.
- Interviews.

The success of most blogs and vlogs is due to personal, bold and original story-telling not mass produced news stories on major television networks and radio stations that are carefully crafted so as not to give too many details, offend, or make the public question anything of significance. Vlogs and blogs are here to stay, but the downside is that many are often censored because they can be very telling or disturbing. There is no freedom of speech on blogs and vlogs about certain topics or fame given if they threaten mainstream media propaganda in some way.

Design something online and your mind will eventually tell you, "What about this...and did you think of looking up that?" One of my ongoing issues I think I will have until the day I die when it comes to Internet activities is how to make something I created better or how to make more money from something I did in the past. If you are like me, as you evolve, you just might want to start a blog or vlog or continue to improve upon the playlists you already have. A playlist is a series of videos or audios that are usually formulated on a media sharing site that specifically addresses a product, service or concern. So you might watch a group of them in one sitting or if you are a creator you may come up with a group of videos and upload in segments.

Family History

There is no need to be curious anymore about a family member when there are many ancestry sites online that can help with your family genealogy research. To date, Ancestry.com is the fastest growing and most trusted website online when it comes to family history. You can also submit a DNA sample and get connected with relatives from around the world if you so choose.

Check out other family history websites by searching the keyword term "family history websites." Since many of these ancestry sites charge fees, you can also seek information for free utilizing various "public record" websites around the web. Put the name of your city or state and include your desired words like: relative's name, school, location, etc. For instance, "birth record" "public records" "cemeteries" "slavery records" "immigrant records" "social security index" "united states census report."

If you want to find available newspaper articles, yearbooks, and other similar information, type the relative's name and any details about the person. For instance, "Jane Doe Jones Elementary School ABC award 1981."

Do keep in mind that sometimes no results will be found since many records are still offline. You will need to make arrangements to receive a copy of the material you might be looking for. Many records can be ordered online. Search for the name of the relative and then include the words, for instance, "John Doe order birth certificate." A long list of websites will show up so that you can order your document. However, shop around, because some sites charge much.

If you are interested in delving deep into researching family history, I suggest you check out my book *Genealogy X: What to Expect When Researching Family History* by Nicholl McGuire it has many tips about how to overcome the brick wall that tends to happen when you think you can't research anymore as well as how to communicate with relatives in order to get quality stories from them and more.

Writers

Lots of tools are online for writers from dictionaries to word count software. Whatever your offline software lacks, you are sure to find it on the Internet. Some freebie software that come with your computer may not have spell correction tools or templates, but if you go online you can find not only those things, but free graphics, moveable icons to include in your documents, and fun stuff to make your presentations stand out. So take a look around for samples and templates of whatever it is you are trying to create and let that imagination of yours run wild! Keyword searches: "writing tools" "word processing software" "mind maps" (helps with planning a book or screenplay) "story templates" "how to write a speech" "websites for writers."

Music

When it comes to listening to music, you can do that on the Inter-net. There are also many ways to create your own personal playlist which might consist of all your favorite entertainment or a specific genre. There are various ways that you can still hear a favorite tune and capture it to be played over and over again. You will need an audio player. There are many providers. You will also need to know where you want your music to be downloaded i.e.) a portable listening device, saved on your computer or on CD. If you really want to experience great music from your computer to your speakers live, simply search "how to connect computer to audio speakers or stereo system."

Music lyrics

Now what was that singer saying again? You no longer have to play a song over and over again to figure out what words they are saying. Just type some of the lyrics of the song and include additional information like the musician's name and a site like Lyrics.com or others will help you figure out your favorite song lyrics.

Discover New Music and Purchase

There are plenty of undiscovered musicians on the Internet and you can find them by searching "indie" and then add the musical genre of your choice. You can also download music legally at many music sites, just include the words in the search engine "buy music downloads" and .com sites like: Pandora, Amazon Cloud Player and Apple iTunes will show up. Also, check out some popular department and bookstores online that also sell music downloads. You can find new music recordings on video sites like YouTube. You can also sample music before you buy when you put the name of an artist and the album title in the search engine.

Create Your Own Music

Maybe you are beginning to tire of listening to other people's creative mixes and songs. If so, learn how to make your own beats, musical scores, and more. You can search "music creator" "music maker" or "recording studio software" download free trials.

After the trial expires, many sites will require you to pay for the software in order to get the full use of it.

You may have your own music sitting on a hard drive. Consider making it available in one of the online stores. You can do this quite easily by searching "how to sell music online" if there is a specific store you have in mind, include that store. You will need to make sure the audio quality is good; copyrights are legitimate, excellent artwork, and more. After you have it uploaded, you will need to search "how to promote your music."

Photographic Memories

What to do with all those photos in boxes, bins, on portable devices, walls, and elsewhere? Well most people share them online. From posting them on social networking pages to inviting contacts to view an online album, there are many ways to share photos. Let's say that someone sent you a photo of a cool event, interesting artwork or a baby, what might you do with it? Most would want to print it out and frame it, but you can do more.

Use quote marks when searching what you want to do with the image (see examples below). The quotes are for highlighting keywords you would use to find the websites that offer the service or product you want. Simply put those in your search engine. Don't forget to add words like: "top" "best" "on sale" to help narrow your options. Include a specific company name if you know of one. For instance, if you don't want to print photos from home, search local drug stores and discount stores that will print your photos and have them ready for pick up within the week.

Join a site that will allow you to print photos on mugs, t-shirts, photo books, tote bags, and more. Use keyword phrases like: "turn photos into..." "print photos on..." "put photos on..."

Find a website that will let you share photos online. You can search "online photo albums."

Worried about space on your hard drive and other places? Check out storing photos privately using online storage. Keyword "online storage for images."

Do you have photos of your ancestors? Why not, open an account with Ancestry.com or a similar family history site? Then upload favorite photos for your distant relatives to view. You can scan them or take photos of them with a camera and then connect camera to computer. Search "how to upload photos from digital camera" or "how to upload photos from phone" If you received photos via email or elsewhere search "how to download photos" then include the way you received the photos. For example, search "how to download photos from Facebook"

What about taking photos and displaying them as works of art? There is much "photo editing software" that can take a dull photo and turn it into a master piece!

Learn more about what you can do with your photos by searching "unique ways to use photos."

So do check out free image hosting, more ways to share your photos easily and fun ways to edit them online or via your portable device. Many people upload their photos to social networking sites and elsewhere. Others create slideshows and share via video services.

Things you can do with your photos online include:
1. Wall posters
2. Banner ads
3. Book covers
4. Icons
5. Apps

6. Video game creations

7. Images in cartoons, short films, and related media

8. Brag books

9. Online and offline photo albums

10. Sell online or share freely on sites that need high quality stock photos and illustrations.

11. Participate in online contests. Baby photograph sub-missions are often in demand.

12. Display on blogs

13. Use as channel art on a video or social networking page

14. Professional headshots are often used for business pro-files

15. Mobile sharing

16. Dating sites

Sometimes people enjoy photography so much that they create entire websites showcasing their many images. Others will open stores and have their images displayed on various items from iPhone covers to games. Since the gaming industry is big business, some websites know how much people love playing video games so they offer features where you can upload photos of yourself, favorite images and more. It is quite fun to see your own face in a character. Simply keyword search "upload your photo games" or "upload photo fun picture game."

When considering a website that caters to photo sharing, check out the reviews of the top 10 sites. You can do this by using the keyword phrase "best photo sharing websites" or "reviews of top 10 photo sharing sites."

Videos and Slideshows

Most of us have already watched videos online. But for those who haven't (which is hard to believe), there are many websites that will allow you to submit your home videos to their websites and some will offer opportunities to make money, participate in con-tests, or help businesses as mentioned in another chapter. Old home videos can be transferred to files easily created for uploading to the Internet for public view. If you don't know how to do this, search "how to upload videos."

People enjoy watching videos made by real people. A practical home video on something useful will draw plenty of attention. Funny videos of babies, pets, and children are often shared on social networking sites and blogs. Sometimes people will upload videos because family members are distant. In this way, relatives can keep one another in the know about the latest happenings.

If you're interested in watching personal videos of those in your local or surrounding communities, you can surf the Internet for "video sharing websites" then include your city or state. Once you are on the site, include the topic you are interested in and look up other cities if you prefer. You will be required to register at the website if you desire to upload your own personal videos. You will also need to purchase necessary equipment or seek a photo service that will help you transfer your old home videos (like VHS) to a compatible format for the Internet. Search "how to transfer VHS to DVD" or whatever other way you would like to see your videos displayed.

If you are interested in making a simple slideshow, most likely you already have software on your computer. Windows Movie-maker is one of the more popular and easy to use programs. Check to see what other movie editing programs is available to meet your needs. There are many videos online that teach you how to create your own slideshows and movies. To learn more, keyword search: "how to make slideshows for Internet" or "how to make videos for Internet."

Copyrights, Trademarks

Any images, videos and photos you upload online may be avail-able to others to re-use. You can protect your work. Keyword search: how to protect images from theft or related keyword terms. Specific searches would include: "how to protect photography online" "how to protect slideshow" ...audio, music, etc. You can also register your work look up United States copyright and learn more about trademarks and other similar things.

Website Building

Someone tells you, "With all that you do, you should have a web-site!" Well these days it isn't as hard as you might think, time consuming, but not hard. There are plenty of sites that offer free services and provide templates. The process is so simple all one has to do is fill in the blanks. Since companies are being built everyday to service this need, you can find out about some by typing "wordpress site builder" "website preset layouts" and "free diy websites."

First, plan out what you would want on your website. To help with your design, search for other websites in your industry. Notice the layout and the kinds of things these companies offer to visitors. Next, you will want to note your observations and then attempt to design your website in a way that is professional, captivating, and best represents your brand. Once you have your ideas written down, start looking for sites that offer free website building services if you have no budget, but you have the skills to create it or keyword search: "free website templates for..." then include your title or business category. However, if you are a seasoned business, you might want to search for a company that will assist you with building your website, so that you can concentrate on other things. Search "website building services" If it is a simple website page that you want with no frills, you just might be lucky enough to find someone willing to create it on Fiverr or a similar site.

When it comes to marketing your business, you can find people through Fiverr if you are budget conscious. Keyword search: top marketing companies online if money is not a problem. You can also put in what service you need in the search engine and then include a price you are willing to pay. Some things to consider before you create your site:

1. What is the purpose of your website or page?

2. What search engine friendly keywords will you use in the name, title, description, headers, etc.? What is the competition currently using or not using?

3. Is the name of the site catchy, simple, and hints to what it is about?

4. Have you checked to see if the url address you have in mind is available as a dot com? (Check out web hosting services).

5. Do you already have a site you could simply redirect to a suitable name? (GoDaddy is one place you can check--it has been around for a long time.)

6. Do you have images prepared, list of names, products, services, and cost?

7. Do you have an about us page, contact information, policies, and more?

Business expenses will rack up, so be sure you have enough money to pay contractors if you should come to a bump in the road when it comes to building your site. Enlist the help of others more knowledgeable than you to help with the website design, content, marketing, and other details. Be sure you are representing your brand well. Have professional shots done of yourself and if you have a brick and mortar location get that photo taken as well.

When selecting individuals to help with your site, check to see that they have completed projects you can view. Find out if others were satisfied with their work. Compare their prices to others on the web. Read contracts thoroughly and don't sign anything you don't understand. The more revisions you request from contractors, additional features, and items on your site, the more money!

Audio

Download audio books to your iPhone, Android, Windows Phone, Kindle or any other mobile device you have or if you are the old school type, just download to your computer. There are many websites that offer free audio books, free samples of audio, and you can also listen to audio within moving or still slideshows. One popular site that is known for having an extensive collection of audio books is Audible.com.

There are so many ways to use audio. The traditional way is to simply listen to it through your radio. Yet, the Internet has made it easy to listen to any genre of music from around the world through your computer speakers. Now if you don't want to listen, what more can you do with audio?

You might have come across old cassettes, CDs, and other products used to record audio in an attic, basement or in a drawer. Why not share those voices with others? There are many devices that can transfer the audio anywhere you would like. But of course, you will need to download software so that the audio will be available on your mobile devices and the Internet.

So let's say you want a funny conversation between relatives that was recorded on cassette long ago to be transferred on your listening device or in a video you would need to take the audio cassette, place it in a device that plays it. Then obtain the connections so that your computer or some other device will attach to it. Lastly, you transfer the recording into the software program that turns it into an mp3/mp4. There are videos around the web that will assist you through this process as well as how-to articles. Keyword search: "how to transfer audio cassette to mp3." You will perform similar searches with any old recordings. You can do the same with vinyl records, 8 tracks and more.

Books

There are so many ways to read a book. Printed books were supposed to be a thing of the past according to some critics when e-books came along; however, with so many ways to purchase them, they won't be going anywhere anytime soon. I enjoy reading books, so to have so many options to read them is a wonderful thing!

I like how smart these websites have become when it comes to providing repeat customers with suggested media based on interests. So if you scroll through a certain genre and then make a purchase, you are sure to see an advertisement and information on the site related to your preference. Amazon.com and others have many selections of literature and fiction, foreign language, religious, business, money, and romance books. You can download them to your mobile device, computer or order your books the traditional way. Some websites provide their customers with space for their personal libraries where they can maintain and organize their items without immediately downloading them.

Let's say that you know others who enjoy reading like you do, there are websites where you can share the books you are reading or have read with others. This is a good way to connect with people online. You can check out their book lists, receive suggested titles or share a few of your own. One popular site is Goodreads.com

Now when it comes to staying on top of the latest trending books, you can keyword search "top books..." and include the genre. You can also visit the sites where you purchase books and search for popular titles.

If you are interested in creating a tome, there are many vanity publishers that cost publishers much money to purchase their own products. So do shop around if you are interested in creating a photo, nonfiction, fiction, anthology, or something similar. I have some products I created using Createspace.com for self publishers. One of my books on the site is *Tell Me Mother You're Sorry*. You can check out how your profile will look on their site and feel free to purchase a copy of my book.

I also have books and basic journals on Blurb.com for those who still enjoy putting pen to paper like myself. On that site, bookmaker software is available for download to your computer. Nevertheless, if you don't want to publish your own book, you can keyword search for "traditional publishing houses." You can also enlist my help or search "book publishers" "ghost writers" or "virtual assistants" to get started on your book. I consult part-time for people interested in publishing their memoirs. See my contact information.

eBooks

One modern way to get your story in front of the masses is by electronic or digital format (e-book) in addition to traditional publishing. E-books are the least expensive to get volumes of work on the Internet for people to read. There are many "e-book libraries" (perform a keyword search) that house numerous books. You can download them freely. You can also search "e-books directories" and "free e-book downloads." E-books tend to be far cheaper than printed books, but there are those that cost just as much if not more than some books in the same genre.

I created my e-books on Smashwords.com. This is a self-publishing platform that is one of the most popular to date. There is no software available on their site to help create an e-book from start to finish as of this writing. One has to write and format his or her book using word processing software then the file is uploaded to the site. Smashwords has a handy guide to help you learn about how to format an e-book. You can view some of my creations on the site for a bit of inspiration search "Nicholl McGuire." Free samples are available.

Consider checking out the newest e-book related tools to help with cover designs, formats, images, marketing, sales, and other ways you can take your e-book to the next level.

Fun Stuff with Books

Sometimes reading is just not good enough for some of us creative types. There is so much stuff to do online. Why would some-one not take advantage of wanting to learn more? I share some of my self-publishing experience online via video. You can keyword search "Nicholl McGuire self publishing" or search my YouTube page (youtube.com/nmenterprise7) for the video.

You can enhance your reading experience in so many ways by doing things such as:

1. Using an online highlighter to mark interesting points.

2. You can use your mobile device features to: make notes, book mark, favorite sections, etc.

3. You can look for book app tools to help with organizing material, comprehension, note-taking, and more.

4. You can create a video talking about the book you read.

5. You might feel inspired by the content you read and want to design artwork.

6. Maybe you don't have time to read the whole book you chose, search for cliff notes.

7. You can send communication out to your network about a book or visit a site where you can display your favorite reads.

Create a blog, keep an online diary, or record audio about the book, but whatever you choose to do with the book, have fun doing it!

Home Design

Whether you live in an apartment or home, there is so much on the Internet to inspire you to decorate, rearrange furniture or declutter. You might have already searched for specific items to beautify your residence or purchase new appliances online. But how about using the Internet to build your own virtual house if you live in an apartment, but plan on buying a home one day? What about checking out home designs and floor plans to improve your exterior and interior?

Many television shows have episodes on their websites that assist with everything from kitchen and bath design to landscaping. So if you missed something on TV you will most likely find it uploaded on the 'Net.

One of the things I like to do is check out the before and after images of home designs. I also like watching decorating and organizing tips. Some sites are interactive and you can find those by keyword searching "interactive home design tools." You can also search for "virtual room designer" include a store name and see what some of them have to offer online when it comes to home design. You can print out the layout of your desired room and then get to work making your dream happen. There are sites for children to get started with home design as well.

I conduct specific searches based on what my needs are so for instance, if I want something for the kitchen or I am interested in changing a room around then I would search "living room design" "living room organizing" "how to organize living room furniture."

Now when it comes to organizing everything from socks in a drawer to tools in the garage, some of the best tips come from novice organizers. I have visited video sites, popular magazine websites, and blogs to get tips. You can also find a variety of home organizing products and watch buyers use them on video sites. But if you don't want to brave the task of organizing your home, there are many professionals available for hire.

I have visited sites that offer certified apartment maintenance classes. You can also research for local classes offered at some popular stores that sell home merchandise.

But maybe you have a dream to start a business, obtain employment in a certain field or you plan to invent something? Take your exploration to the next level by searching for information on "how to start a business..." include what your interest might be in home interior design, apartment maintenance, property management, commercial real estate, etc.

If you are interested in creating a home invention, you will enjoy looking at the latest ones by keyword searching: "wacky home inventions" "inventions..." then include the current year. You can get a free invention kit and also learn about the process by searching for "new invention idea" "free invention kit" "how to patent invention" "new inventions advice" Visit sites that provide tutorials and tips without feeling pressured to get register with a company. Also, research the company first before submitting your idea and don't agree to anything without checking with an attorney first. Search "tips inventors law" and learn much about trademarks, copyright, etc.

Garden and Landscaping

Sometimes people view things on TV or notice beautifully designed landscapes as they drive. Plenty of observers hope to duplicate efforts one day. But you can turn that hope into reality today! One suggestion to consider is list the name of what you think encompasses the layout. What might the flowers be called that you saw? Describe color and shape in the search engine and see what comes up. What is the type of items used to create the landscape effect? Search video to see how some designs are performed. You might want to Google the address/location to see if there are current photos of the layout.

Visit the websites of those television shows you enjoy watching. You will find a lot will include a list of what to buy to get desired results. They also tend to have the video from the show on the site. But if not, try YouTube. Many old television shows end up on video sites around the web. Include the show name and a couple of words related to it.

Don't sleep on blogs of fellow gardeners and people who enjoy decorating the outside of their homes. There are useful tips on those sites. You can add your interest in the search engine then include the word "blogs" and a host of them will show up in the search engine. If you know the name of the person who created it, include that name too.

You can find online encyclopedias on a variety of subjects as well. Popular home improvement stores often share tips and classes on and offline, so also check out their sites too. The Home Depot website includes advice on home design, gardening, landscaping, and more. They include lists of things you will need for your project. It is also a great site for finding out what is new as well.

If you enjoy checking out the latest home improvement trends, type your interest in the search engine and then add "trends" to it. So if you want to find out the latest man-made colors in a certain flower, you can do this by entering the name of the flower then adding keywords "new colors" or "types." Do this with latest landscaping techniques, gardening strategies and include the year. If you enjoy articles they will show up, but if you don't want to read and rather watch a video then include the word "videos" in your search as well. For example, "new landscape designs 2017 videos."

Online Video

You may not have bothered to do much with online video. How-ever, it can be one of the most important services that you use on the Internet especially when you are having trouble making, creating, building or fixing something. YouTube is the most popular to date. You can search for everything from the latest music video to how to cook a favorite recipe. However, maybe you know a few things you can teach others. You can upload your own video on the site. You can also share video of family events and talk about things that matter to you. Use the filter function on the site and you can sort videos based on day, week, month, etc.

But what if you want to find professionally made videos of a specific interest? That's when you will search using a broader term like "online videos" then include what it is that you are looking for by adding a company name or words like "doctor" "professional" or "instructor" in the major search engines rather than exclusively looking for video within YouTube. For instance, I want to learn more about cutting hair, so I would put in the Bing search engine box, "how to cut African American hair videos + professional stylists."

Talk via video - Video Chat

You can video chat (VOIP service) with anyone from around the world. Connect with relatives and friends via video. Search what services are available to date for free or are inexpensive to use. Check that your computer has a quality web cam, since you will be viewed once you make the call.

Live stream

This is a video platform that allows people to broadcast using a computer with a webcam and the Internet. So if you want to watch a video live, you will be able to do so through any website that makes live streaming possible. This service is popular with online churches, radio hosts, and teachers.

Webcam

Plug in your webcam or use the one already available on a computer and you never know where you might end up. There are many uses for webcams. Think of some interesting things you can do with yours. If you need a better webcam, try searching "top 10 webcams for..." include the current year to see what comes up.

Here is a list of some things I have done over the years with video:

1. Created slideshows and included still images as well as clips of old family videos.

2. Used a live streaming video service to broadcast a holiday experience.

3. Filmed short clips to use for marketing products and services.

4. Recorded my children's early developments.

5. Sent video via email for others to view.

6. Found images online and put them together for research projects.

7. Used video to illustrate personal views about controversial subject matter.

Consider using video for job interviews, sharing valuable data about something you don't want to read entirely online, teach something new, and explore new places.

3 Business

There are countless things you can do online to take your business or someone else's to the next level like: manage productivity, increase profits, hire additional help, expand, and promote goods and services. You can also keep track of many essential tasks daily, weekly and monthly. With so many useful tools on the Internet to help individuals and businesses, you simply can't go wrong!

Apps

In your quest to want to do more with your online experiences, you will find that daily apps are being used to make many lives simpler. So what kind of apps might be worth downloading from the App store or Google play? Well it all depends on what your needs are. Before beginning your research on apps (watch becoming over-whelmed visiting site after site), first list problems you might want to solve regarding a business, home, church, and elsewhere. For instance, let's say you have the following common issues:

1. Problem trying to remember birthdays.

2. Having trouble keeping track of children's chores and allowance money.

3. Sometimes you need a flashlight when it's dark.

4. At times you need to measure something quickly.

5. You might not always know your family's schedule like: doctor's appts., days your partner works, keeping up with children's activities or even forgetting to water the plants or feed fish.

6. Maybe you get bored cooking the same meals sometimes. When shopping, you forget needed ingredients for recipes.

7. You need to scan a document, but aren't near a scanner.

Situations like these and more arise. You have that handy phone, android, notebook, or other electronic device, what kind of apps might help you?

So for those of you who wonder how apps might be beneficial to you, think about the following:

What do you typically do during the day or night? Could an app with some kind of reminder help you with things like: taking medicine, scheduling activities, performing daily tasks, meeting relatives and friends, or participating in errands?

Here is a list of ideas that many people already use mobile and computer apps for:

1. Hair and nail appointments.

2. Reminders such as take birth control, visit doctor, assist others, etc.

3. Keep up with their children's tasks.

4. Read magazines and other media while they wait for others.

5. Play games.

6. Apartment shop.

7. Find locations.

8. Post information on social media pages.

9. Keep up with celebrities.

10. Write.

11. Create music.

12. Collaborate with staff.

13. Connect with friends.

14. Meet new friends.
15. Date online.
16. Check out photos.
17. Keep up with allowance money given to children.
18. Budget finances.
19. Learn about latest movies.
20. Share documents.
21. Get directions.
22. Get traffic updates.
23. Stay up-to-date on home security.
24. Measure things.
25. Perform complex math computations.
26. Learn more about colleges and universities.
27. Find out the latest job postings.

Of course, you could think of many more apps to kill boredom, make best use of your time, communicate, discover new things, etc. In general, apps are great to have on any portable device, because they make it easier to do things by simply pushing, sliding, pinching, or tapping with your fingers or stylus tool (a pen with a rubber tip that helps with typing and selecting things). When you need to look up something you can just tap on the Google app. Want to keep up with sales at your favorite stores and coupon deals, download the apps.

Apps simplify the process of going on the Internet especially when you are out and about. Rather than typing in a URL address like www.google.com every time you want to look up something, you download the app and it is always on your device. You will also find that Google apps are many, so search through their choices and select an app based on your need. However, keep in mind the more apps you download, the more storage you are taking up especially on a smart phone or android if you don't have much space. It doesn't take long before you will notice a message telling you that the phone can no longer be backed up or it can't accept your request to take anymore pictures or videos. So be sure you download the app you need not what you think you might need.

For those of you who tend to think beyond the box and have a few ideas of your own when it comes to apps, you might want to search for what has already been done or something similar to your thought. I wouldn't recommend giving the search engine too many details about your app ideas, because many individuals look to the Internet for thoughts on creating their next inventions. As mentioned earlier, do check with companies that will help you design your inventions. Also, seek reference materials on how to create apps, market them, and sell them to major corporations.

Business Services

With many businesses on the Internet, there is a lot of money being made providing services to help companies maintain websites, build their brands, enhance their products, attract more customers, and do other things. When it comes to marketing services, there is much networking online similar to what goes on offline. Sites are frequented by competitors and alliances, details are noted, and information gets passed along to leadership to improve their brand. How you choose to network online is left up to you. There are numerous ways to do so from commenting to emailing anyone who has contact information about your product or service. However, keep in mind when you start connecting with businesses, you will need to make the time to answer emails, reply to comments, like, subscribe, supply information, and frequently post to your social media pages and keep other online profiles current.

I personally found that conducting searches on how to market my business has been most helpful. Don't limit your searches to popular engines like Google and Yahoo. Broaden your searches to social media and book-marking sites as well as others to find out what people like, need, and can't live without.

Seek contact information on websites you like to visit and connect with the owners about your business needs. Check company sites for blogs and visit video sites for useful data about target consumers and businesses.

I have sent letters to webmasters and others on numerous sites from email to social media letting them know what I can offer them and how much I like their sites. Let these people know when you have shared their links, added them to your pages, referred them to others, and things you have done directly and indirectly related to their site. You never know where your connections might lead. Keep track of your contact list using an online or offline spreadsheet or database. If you don't know how to communicate effectively with professionals online, do search for "how to write business letters" and check out samples. Rewrite to fit your needs.

List your most important tasks each day you need to complete and set monthly goals. Before long, you will grow your business and gain interested followers who don't mind doing business with you. If you are new to marketing, you will find countless sites providing insight on how to track your business growth and measure the impact your advertising efforts are making, where to find needed information to determine who is your audience, and how might you improve communications and other services between your company and customers.

Take a moment to create a list of keyword phrases related to your business that people might be talking about on various social media pages. Search for things like: the top 25 social networking sites and see what the visitors are saying about products related to your business. Also, check out the top 10 competitors in your industry. Make time to search and comment on blogs, you will find much valuable information from the people who might possibly can use your services.

By connecting with bloggers and others via their postings and including your website url (Internet website address) you are gaining additional connections that will help your site's ranking in Google. Link rank is essential because you want people to see your business when they type keywords related to your industry. Visit forums and other places people ask questions. Supply them with your answers and request they get in touch with you.

Social Media

Individuals and businesses are using a variety of social media mediums to gain popularity and also tools to help with the back office stuff. Professionals organize projects online, automate mundane tasks like tweets, use tools to help with gaining follow- ers, and autobots for commenting, responding to questions, etc. Search "social media tools" include the name you want to find out the latest product information. Also, check out the latest schedul- ers that will automatically post on other sites besides Twitter. Add the name of the website you want to automate and then include "scheduler."

Search Engine Optimization (SEO)

This is a service provided to many businesses that are in need of certain website enhancements so that they are better ranked in the search engines. With SEO, you will discover ways that website developers make effective websites that put them at number one for specific keywords. Learn more about "search engine optimization" and have your website analyzed for any weaknesses that could be preventing your site from being noticed by the search engines and how to fix those errors.

SEO Tools

When it comes to marketing your business online it will also help to know the tools that professionals use to build online traffic and a presence. Look up online tools for link building, rank tracking, technical SEO, content optimization, keyword research, backlink analysis. All of which there are numerous videos, infographics (visuals), articles, webinars, and more for further study. Some tools are for free, paid and freemium (limited features for a set period of time).

Marketing

From email campaigns to link swapping, there are so many ways to get the word out about your business online. I often see online business cards that are sent directly into my email or shared via text. If you are interested in business cards and other promotional materials, search specific keywords and then add what type you might want include a color, style or theme in the search engine.

You can visit sites that have do-it-yourself online business cards. These tend to be used in email signatures, social media postings, and attached to other forms of communication including social media profiles.

Once an individual or business builds a network via a social networking page, blogs, website or another medium, the marketing of products and services is a cinch--actually selling is a different story. The process of building your online presence is time-consuming and it can take a long time before you see any steady traffic to your site. Some tasks you might start or get someone else to do for you to help promote your services or products include:

1. Leaving comments on other websites and blogs with a link to your website.

2. Content writing and article distribution on major sites in your industry.

3. Set up pod-casting where you or others are talking about things related to your site.

4. Create e-books.

5. Voiceovers for commercials.

6. Media interviews.

7. Newsletters or online magazines.

You can find someone doing almost anything to help with marketing on sites that list sellers and virtual assistants who are experienced in many areas. I would start with your specific need and then include the cost you are willing to pay and the city you are located. There are sites that will connect you with professionals but some of these businesses do charge fees. To date, there is a site called, Fiverr.com where you can get workers for $5 and up and others who provide $10 services. But if Fiverr doesn't exist anymore or the name changes search as previously mentioned for your specific need. Check to see if the site has customer comments about each seller. Watch for sellers who are overseas and those who provide vague information about where they will post your product or service information. Unfortunately, there are those who will provide "proof" they have performed a task, but that so-called proof isn't always what it appears to be and sometimes there is no way to verify that the work was really done like they claim. Some sellers use fake screenshots and others tend to be quite pushy about wanting high ratings even when their work doesn't deserve it.

So if I needed someone to create a logo for me, I would keyword search "need seller to help with logo" or "logo design services." I would add the cost I am willing to pay just to see what comes up. But if I change my mind and want to create my own logo, I would search "logo generators" or "how to create logos." I would also perform other searches seeking someone in my local area as well. Once I found a site, I would look for any contact information, terms and conditions, and other pertinent information. You can perform a search in your main search engine then include the name of the company and add Better Business Bureau, customer reviews, etc.

When we think of those unexpected emergencies, rise and fall of revenue, and other business blues, the ease of being able to tell your audience quickly via the Internet about your business updates is beneficial. You can do many things to generate interest in your business such as: request donations using crowd sourcing efforts, post banner ads, consult with others about a link exchange, establish affiliates to help with marketing, use online video, host an online radio show, purchase online ad space, build additional websites and blogs, enlist the help of writers to create articles, press releases, books, etc. There are so many ways to tell others you exist.

I discovered many small businesses by visiting eBay and similar sites. Through my research efforts and spotting ads along the right side of my screen I was lured to little known businesses through specific product advertising. I have also clicked on ads while visiting a website, blog and watching videos. Although I don't do this often it has been an attention-grabber for me. But the most popular way that still works is direct email advertising. If I notice a sale or bargain on something I like, I will click on the email before sending it to junk or trash.

Of course, marketing services isn't the only thing that businesses need. You can find sellers doing many things such as: programming, graphics and design, video, animation, music and audio, and other services.

Can you think of some other things you might need to help grow your business? Here is a list to get you going. What you aren't familiar with, take a moment to search for it.

- Social media page design.
- Cartoons and caricatures
- Banner ads
- Business cards and stationery
- Illustration
- T-shirts, pens, mugs, and more.
- Invitations
- Website design.
- Photoshop editing.
- Book Covers
- Logo Designs

- Presentations
- Web business cards

Search for things like: "book promotion," "schedule tweets," "schedule Pinterest pins," "social book-marking," and other useful things to help with marketing. I assist individuals with various tasks, feel free to contact me at nichollmcguire@gmail.com.

Meetings and Marketing Campaigns

There are many professionals that will help with building email campaigns, subscriber lists, online appointment setting, Internet staff meetings and collaboration, scheduling events, writing press releases, and more. With so much online software to help with daily tasks, there is sure to be something or someone that saves both time and money. One way to find out what you might be missing is to perform general searches and browse websites.

For instance, if I want to find out what is the newest photo edit- ing software I will just type that into my browser. Maybe I am curious about what competitors might use to keep track of sales, clients, or traffic to a website. I would put the name of the industry or company and then include what it is I want to know. You can do this when you visit a video website like YouTube. This way you can see how the software performs, the service a company pro- vides to help with marketing efforts, trending tools, and more.

Buying and selling online is a great way to generate income. One can buy from a fellow reseller, mark up items, and then sell to the masses. He or she can then look for another business profes- sional/wholesaler who needs some help moving their products and sell those items through a variety of websites to generate addi- tional revenue. Almost immediately, many sellers have money in their accounts because they post quality items that are useful and in demand.

Buying Online

When it comes to buying products online, it can be tedious and other times quite easy. Sometimes websites upload slowly or malfunction, items run out of stock, or sites simply don't have what you need. But your efforts never are in vain once you get pass all the distractions and land a great deal. I have discovered many bargains simply because I took the time to check out the latest coupon codes and visited some of the sites that offered rebates before I made a purchase. Some of the best places I found deals as well as sold items are as follows. Other websites that are overlooked at times are the following: local thrift stores and bou- tiques, neighborhood blogs and websites, online sites of relatives and friends, and social networking sites. These as well as many others will periodically have special promotions and freebies.

Online Selling

Over the years, I have utilized various websites to create multi- ple income streams such as: online auction sites, personal blogs, classified advertising, and others. Some have been successes and others not so much. Finding a way to make additional money takes time and you will need the motivation and discipline to keep with your resource once you discover it.

I will never forget the day when I realized that I could sell items wholesale via an auction site. I prayed about what to start selling and literally over night, I found something useful and sold literally hundreds of the product. So is it possible to run a small business from home solo? Yes. Can you make enough money to pay the bills? Yes. There are far too many people on the Internet who have been there, done that and still doing some things to increase their wealth.

Online Auctions

You have heard about eBay one of the most popular online auction sites in the world. It is also the easiest website to use to make money quickly. Simply find something in your household, find the category to sell it, take a picture, write something about it, upload the photo, make a few selections regarding payment, provide other details like shipping and handling costs and then you're done!

Most online auction sites operate the same way. If you are looking for one of the best ways to make money online selling merchandise using online auctions is the way to go. However, when you do a search in general for "online auctions," you will find many are not as popular as eBay and don't have the massive traffic that eBay has; therefore, it will take longer to move the product out of your home into someone else's. Besides, when you are just beginning to learn about any website and what it can do for you, you might as well stick with the best. Some websites are better than others because they have learned how to work out a lot of the website glitches, listen to their visitors' ideas and suggestions, make adjustments, and create loyal followers by handling their concerns and more.

The first thing you will want to do is visit the online auction sites and learn as much as you can. You will want to navigate through the pages. Go to the "about us" section of each and the FAQ (Frequently Asked Questions) section, and also look for something on the site usually on the bottom that says, "Contact Us." This way if you have a question, you can call someone who can help.

Online Classified Advertising

Although some will still utilize print media to sell household goods and other things, many sellers find their items are sold much faster via online ads. Craigslist is one of the largest and most popular advertising websites. But there are also social networking and video sites that offer advertising programs. If you have numerous items to sell, take advantage of any online tools that might help with things like posting or pay others to assist.

Build Your Website or Sell Items from Your Own Storefront

Sellers can use pre-existing templates and build their own web-sites simply by googling "free website templates." However, if you don't want to build your own, just keyword search "website developers" or visit an online classified advertising site and search for someone who can build a site for you. Don't pay the individual or company anything until you have seen his or her work and performed a background check. If you aren't up for the challenge of creating a website from scratch, there are online stores that help you create a product and then sell it on their site or elsewhere. You can learn more about this by checking out CaféPress or search "personalized products."

Make Your Blog, Website, YouTube and Social Networking Pages Work for You

Set aside the space to advertise your products or someone else's to your audiences on each of the sites you are affiliated with. You can create advertiser revenue with your blog, website or video. Think of other places that offer opportunities to monetize. Don't waste time signing up for sites that give you nothing for all your hard work.

You can use your various social connections to sell goods. People direct their existing traffic all the time to links where they are selling their own products or someone else's for commission.

Other things people have done to make money online include: downloaded tools and apps that pay users, created fund-raising campaigns to obtain money to get their businesses off the ground (search for things like: "how to organize fund-raising campaign XYZ Company"), sell photographs and other images, flip and sell websites and blogs, contacted individuals and groups and asked for money, participate in online investment programs, and offered a variety of Internet services from writing to website enhancements and promotion. These are doable and successful ways to make money online. Of course, there are many others, so do take some time to research your favorite interest, then visit websites to help you launch your idea(s).

Documents

What I have enjoyed about the Internet when it comes to creating, managing, sharing, and filing documents is the convenience. I am able to find tools available to assist me with writing and editing. I like how easy it is to find and download a word processing software program online, check definitions of words and grammatical structure, seek resources, and do all the things I would have needed many books offline in the past.

Some of the things that are available to make your document preparation process a cinch are available in the form of the following: templates, presentations, tables, outlines, spreadsheets, and video. Let's say you have to prepare a letter but you have trouble writing it. You can research for letter templates based on your needs. So if you need a sales letter for a product or wanted to write a complaint to a company, there are plenty examples to get you started. Chances are someone has written a similar letter. With a template, you can select the format and rewrite the content contained in the sample. If it isn't good enough, you can always seek another template, change the style and reword the information.

When you need to take what is offline in print and present it before an audience, there are so many pre-existing presentations to receive inspiration. How do you want to take your printed draft to another level? Print it in a PDF format and people can view it as an electronic document. The Portable Document Format (PDF) is a file format that is used to present online documents. It is created to be printed and read online. You can also use a printer to view the document offline too. Maybe you prefer to condense the document into a table format or outline it and have people comment on it online.

Slideshows are a popular way to present your writing as well. I have watched writers take entire articles and paste them into individual slides. They include interesting graphics, sometimes sound and the overall presentation is impressive.

Software

There are websites that will allow you to upload documents and encourage others to view them online. Business professionals collaborate via the Internet adding details to documents, commenting and more. Keyword search: "Google documents" to get started or check for "Google documents alternatives" to find similar

Internet programs. You will find various online and offline word processing software programs available. The programs are quite helpful especially when you don't want to download anything to your computer. There are free ones if you have no money to pay for yet another Microsoft Office download. Check for Microsoft Access alternatives (database software), Microsoft PowerPoint alternatives (slideshows/presentations) and Excel alternatives (spreadsheets) software.

Files

Say so long to all those file drawers, binders, folders, albums and more that once held so many of your documents. You can turn every one of your keepsakes into digital files and store them online. It is so easy to do and professional looking once complete. To help you start your journey, check out videos on "how to trans- fer files to PDF videos."

Outlining

If it has been awhile since you used an outline before you wrote something, just keyword search "how to create an outline" or view some based on whatever your need is by checking for "im- ages" in the search box or type "Google images" or "image of outline for..." in another search engine include the kind of outline you need if you want to be more specific.

Reference and Index Tools

Forgot how to create a bibliography for a research paper or in- dex your material for a book? No problem. There are tools avail- able to help you format correctly. For example, keyword searches: "book indexing software" or "bibliography generator." For other needed items, type in the text and then include the word "tools" or you can always put "how to..." then include what it is you need to learn or re-learn.

Other Documents

Here is a list of some things you might not have thought about in awhile when it comes to preparing various documents:

1. How to create a manuscript
2. How to format a recipe book
3. How to write a book
4. How to create a brochure
5. Business card software
6. Greeting card software
7. How to create a screenplay
8. How to write an essay
9. How to write a product review
10. Calendar making software
11. How to create a job application
12. How to write a rental property lease agreement
13. How to write a business grant
14. How to format a resume
15. How to write and format a query letter

Education

It is almost too easy to learn something new nowadays. If you have some idea what you like to do, you should have no problem finding material to learn more about your interest online. You will also want to keep your eyes open for any license, certificate, and job you might be able to obtain as a result.

For children there are printable worksheets, online games, and other tools to help with learning. Teens and adults will find similar things depending on what your interests might be. So let's say, you are seeking to find out what your life's purpose might be. Well besides meditating, fasting or attending a church, you can also take an online career assessment test and a personality quiz.

Based on those results, you can start researching what best suits you. If you were to find out you were analytical, logical and have many other attributes that demonstrate attention to detail, leader-ship skills, etc. you may be a good match for a job in finance working at a bank. Next, you would start searching for what types of classes you might need to enhance your skills. Whatever the career field, you will notice in the search engines suggested online schools or colleges, articles, books, and videos of popular teachers and advisers.

The following is a checklist of things to do to add to your educational endeavors:

1. Do you know what you like to do? Search career assessment tools, career aptitude test, or career development.

2. If you know what you enjoy learning, think what classes have you taken so far? Type "classes in..." then seek out additional classes you might need. So let's say you knew a friend who wanted to become a nurse, she might have taken math, biology, and other related courses. So you would type "classes in nursing" "classes in nursing school" "night classes in nursing" "online classes in nursing" Do the same for your desired job.

3. Have you watched any video about the profession? You can get the latest video by searching for related employment and then filter by day, week, month, or year.

4. Do you know the latest salary range? Search "salary his-tory" "salary calculator" "salary comparison"

5. Are there any classes being offered locally? Type city/state and learn what schools in your area can help. Note: Search whatever you will need to work in the profession and then include words like: free classes, discounted classes, affordable classes, online certification and similar searches to save money.

6. Any job fairs and other events coming to the area? You can find out through local government sites, Chamber of Commerce and visiting libraries. In addition, check out local newspapers, and call nonprofit organizations that help with employment by obtaining contact information via the online yellow pages.

Add to the checklist as you learn more about how you can ob-tain more higher learning. Make an appointment with a career counselor who can offer you guidance.

Online Tutoring and Teaching

Tutors are readily available online to help you via video, webi-nars, sharing documents and more. If you are already skilled in some-thing, there are sites that can help you become a tutor. You can prepare presentations of you teaching something then upload those videos and sell them online. You can learn more about teaching online by searching "Get paid to teach online..." include what it is that you want to offer your students.

Maybe a degree, a career or job is not something you need right now, but you just want to enhance your skills, learn a new hobby, or find out more about what others do. There are many ways to do this. Besides keyword searches, you could go directly to a site that you may have seen advertised on television or in print. Some of these websites have questionnaires and quizzes right on their sites you can test. Others will have resources that direct you to additional information including offline programs.

I have personally visited sites recommended to me by a career professional through an employment agency. For years, I was registered on a site that had online tests to help me improve on my word processing and administrative skills. I was also introduced to other software programs as well on the same site. If you are interested in learning more to improve your administrative skills, contact a career employment office or a staffing agency and find out what they have to offer online to advance professionals.

Fun Educational Stuff

I enjoy watching videos about all sorts of things I didn't know existed. For instance, what if you wanted to learn more about a favorite hobby? You turn on your computer, open your Internet window and then search for a video about the thing you were curious about. But why stop there? How about checking for the most recent article about it after watching the video? Type the subject and today's date in the search engine. Then after reading the article, search for a suggested printed book or audio book and then make an online purchase. But you still aren't finished.

How about looking for an online group to join who talks about your hobby at least once a week or start a community discussion about it? Afterward maybe you might search some blogs and read what people, just like you, have done to make things even more interesting when it comes to your favorite hobby. But don't cut off that computer just yet. What are people saying about it on Twitter or other social networks? What images have they collected about your interest? Hobbyists probably have some links posted, so why not click on those? But you don't want to go now, do you? Are there classes about your hobby available on or offline for you to join, why not search for them too?

What you just read is a chain of events that can take on any given subject all because of the Internet. This is how people take their online experiences to the next level and the next and become more and more knowledgeable about them. Savvy Internet users don't just get on the computer, type a few words, and look at a couple things then go about their days. They make what they learn a part of their lifestyles so that they can get the most from their discoveries.

By doing more with your Internet searches, you are making those experiences much more interesting and useful. You also give yourself a few more things to look forward to in your offline life. For instance, you will anticipate that package coming in the mail that you ordered online. Your forum connections might lead to offline friends. You will learn things you never knew due to classes and group discussions and you might want to get involved in local events. You see, thanks to the Internet, you are getting more out of life!

Here are some suggestions to enhance that wonderful brain of yours that wants to be exercised:

1. Visit sites that offer brain exercises to improve memory, stroke recovery, etc.

2. Take classes online for free or to raise a grade point average.

3. Learn how to play an instrument online.

4. Find out more about local museums, galleries, and special events that educate the public.

5. Search free worksheets and workbooks on...you fill in the blank.

6. Find online tutors for...what subject are you struggling in?

7. Educational games that help with...type what your need or someone else's might be. When I was teaching my children how to read, I looked for educational games to enhance their skills.

8. Look around your environment. What is it that needs to be fixed, but you don't know how to deal with the issue? From relationships to problems with appliances, someone online has advice.

9. Teach yourself a new skill by downloading a software program, e-book, or attending an online class or register at an online university.

10. Take out online library books about anything you are curious about.

11. Create online flash cards to help memorize things.

12. Seek games and puzzles online about your interests.

Employment

The Internet is a playground for the job seeker! There is everything on it to help someone prepare and find a job. You will find samples of cover letters, video tutorials on how to prepare for interviews, dos and don't on what to wear, and how to write and edit your resume for a desired position.

Nowadays professionals join networks to connect with former as well as new employers. They also look for opportunities in the future. To date, Linked In is one of the most popular ones many employees and companies join. There is numerous information on how to properly represent yourself on the site, what postings are appropriate, and how to communicate with others online. You can research this site as well as "Linked In alternatives" and expand your online connections. Some career advisers talk of using your Facebook page to obtain employment as well by giving it a make-over. This is something worth considering since many Human Resources staff are online checking not only for a candidate's accomplishments, but social media pages as well.

If you don't want to use the Internet to help you with your job search, there are plenty of books you can purchase online that promise to help. As a job seeker, the first thing you will want to do is register with the best websites for job seekers in your local area. The more popular the website, the more the competition. Of course, popular doesn't necessarily mean best. Look for job sites in your local area and join their mailing lists. Be sure you have your resume saved on your computer and a hard copy nearby because some of these sites will have you fill out an online form. Keep your name, address and phone private if you don't want just anyone calling you, rather include your email. You will also want to select the kinds of jobs that interest you so that the automated system on each of the sites will only send you emails related to those jobs.

During my job searches I have stumbled across many sites that make it easy to apply online using portable electronic devices. I have also noticed there are numerous sites that help market resumes, but from personal experience, I have found a lot useless. You might register with one career board; see a job online, only to be asked to register for that site, and another and another. So when searching for sites to help with your job search, do take the time to be sure it is not just another mill collecting resumes. The websites that you pay for can be just as bad as the free ones, so be on the look out for the useless ones and the scams.

Here's what you need that will be helpful when it comes to employment:

Fundraising Initiatives

If you want to bypass the do-it-yourself fundraising campaigns, then you can always go with professional agencies that provide fundraising services.

Make Money from Home

Searching for new ways to make additional money is something that I have done annually for a couple decades now. There is always some new business that claims it will give you thousands, but from personal experience, multi-level marketing (MLM) businesses have been a let down over the years. I have made money with them, but I don't like their systems. The fastest and legitimate way I made money was through online selling. You have a product that people want, you post it up on a website that already has much traffic, and if you just happened to be one of a few sellers of that product, practically overnight there is money in your PayPal account. A few popular ways people make passive online income follows.

Survey Participation

Taking online surveys and those via your mobile device are great ways to generate additional income when you are doing nothing more than riding in a car, standing in line, or waiting for someone. Although the pay is pennies on the dollar, it is more than what most banks will give you if you were to place a small amount of money in a savings account.

Reward Programs

Companies will offer incentives to use search engines, shop via select websites, "like" their products, share comments, and more.

You can find out about the successful ones by searching "earn money for online activities...get paid to search...get paid to shop..." as mentioned in the chapter about shopping. You will find that businesses offline have many ways to save online by downloading their apps, joining money-saving programs, and other useful things.

Read Emails

Ads are sent to the users email account. They read the email and then confirm they have reviewed it. If they should click sign up for the program or buy the product advertised then they get some money for doing so.

Play Games and Watch Videos

This is one of the easiest and there are plenty of sites for children 12 years old and up to register. I have a list of sites that you can check out if you are interested in making additional money or points to buy things. Check out my blog Bored? Looking for Things to Do (thingstodobored.blogspot.com).

Get Paid to Search

There are sites that reward you for using their search engines. To date, I personally use Bing. If you would like to join "Search Bing. Earn Free Rewards."

Affiliate Websites

Join an affiliate program through a company selling products and services. These websites look for people to assist with their sales. You can learn more about this by searching "affiliate programs" or "reseller partner program." There are also affiliate marketing and programs directory.

If you have some idea what you want to do then you should have no problem searching for it. But if you are clueless as to how to begin searching for ways to make money, then keyword search: "get paid to...get paid to sell... companies that pay...get paid to create..." You can also search "fun ways to make money...unique ways to make money...things to do to make money...how to make money." Here are some things that people do online to make money:

1. Test video games.
2. Listen to music.
3. Tweet messages.
4. Get paid to like products, services, ads, businesses, etc.
5. Sell digital items, videos and photos.
6. Sell products from home or drop-ship.
7. Become online tutors.
8. Give opinions.
9. Write reviews.
10. Listen to sales calls.
11. Work from home customer service.
12. Graphic design such as visual presentations.
13. Rate or review things.
14. Increase website page views.
15. Make book covers.
16. Design websites.
17. Social bookmark.
18. Link advertising (or ask to link swap for free with others).
19. Create slideshows and videos.
20. Send email.

21. Perform voice-overs.

22. Write music, sing for others, or market new music.

23. Advertise on blog, website, and other places.

24. Create channel art.

25. Write, edit and proof documents, articles, books, etc.

26. Data entry tasks.

27. Design their own products (t-shirts, mugs, posters, etc.)

28. Offer translation services.

29. Transportation services like Uber.

30. Set up slideshows like on My Likes and get paid to market their own as well as others' projects.

If you are looking for more ideas to search on the Internet, I prepared a list on my YouTube channel. If you don't mind performing small tasks online, Clickworker is always looking for workers.

Notice the list I provided doesn't include any get rich quick schemes. Over the years, I met people on and off the Internet that were successful doing the things I mentioned and I also did well over the years selling items and services online too. The money was supplemental for us. There was no getting rich off the payments we received from customers. I enjoyed performing a variety of tasks for individuals and businesses and to date I still offer my virtual assistant services. You can stop by my personal blog nichollmcguiremedia.blogspot.com.

You will find that as you search for ways to make money from home, there will be many sites that will provide a single company and encourage you to join their mailing lists. I have done this and watched my inbox for emails to tell me more about the opportunity. I have also researched the name of the company and visited sites that weren't that popular to check reviews. It is easy for some businesses to pay others to write positive reviews, so this is why I like visiting little known sites. Search "former employee" "ex-employee" "worker" or "member" then add the business name and scroll until you see some unflattering postings. Don't forget to check with the BBB.

Organizing

Consider all of the items you have in your residence like: pens, papers, tools, toys, clothes, shoes, makeup, fragrances, etc. Some things are neatly arranged while others are all over the place. A lot of items you might find with ease others not so much. There are organizers online who perform major makeovers to their homes or make small changes, but whatever you choose to do with your dwelling; the Internet is available to help you meet your goals.

Most likely someone has already done what you are hoping to do and has uploaded a video, wrote an article, or might have recorded a radio show online about it. Simply keyword whatever your intentions might be. Maybe you want to learn to do something better in your home like "organize office space" or find a way to construct something that can help meet personal goals.

Now if you are a reader, you can search e-books, books and other documents about your desired "how-to organize..." topic. Let's say you have little money, but really need to get the project done. Then you would keyword search your interest and then include "free book" or "free pdfs." Oftentimes people will upload files with the PDF extension onto website servers for people to download things like: instructions, books, outlines, reports, etc. So if you can get a diagram or other information online for free, why not try searching for something for free first?

Home Organizing Resources

Now if you have a little money to invest in further educating your-self on your home organizing project, consider online books, apps, or DVDs. You can find media reasonable on Amazon.com. Of course, there are many more websites, so do search "cheap DVDs" or "used books". Always comparison shop, because you might find this kind of media cheaper on eBay or at a local thrift store website.

As for home organizing supplies you will find thousands featured on YouTube in addition to specific room arrangements and decoration ideas. Like Amazon, YouTube seems to be going strong these days. Professionals as well as novices upload videos on the site about a number of things including how to organize things in a drawer to how to declutter a massive home.

If you should want to invent your own item to help with organizing stuff, there are plenty of handymen and women online you will be inspired by. Many organizers and Jack of all Trades types show you how to do everything from wall hangings to shelf units. Simply keyword search "how to build…" and include your desired project. Stores like Ikea and Home Depot are great inspirations on getting your home together!

Work

Whether you have a home office or one elsewhere, it is always interesting to find out how others keep their work areas neat, tidy, and smelling great. You can search for new ways to maximize your workplace setting like "how to organize work cubicles productivity."

Be more productive and look for recent developments in your industry along with the kind of media you would like to view the information. Add a competitor's name to your search (depending on the subject matter) and notice how they build traffic to their site. Then search for "ideas on increasing website traffic." You can check out useful material on my comprehensive blog mentioned previously in this book Workplace Problems and Solutions (workplaceproblems.blogspot.com).

School or College

When it comes to school or higher learning, whether you or some-one you know is a student, he or she will need to be organized. Let's say the issue is a small one like "how to organize a back-pack" or a binder, there are volumes of videos on this subject. Maybe you have trouble keeping track of everything you need to do. Check out apps as well as online computer software that can help with keeping up with one's schedule.

Sometimes knowing what to buy, how to put it together or arrange items can be so frustrating. So when directions are unclear, as most of us know, there is always the Internet. When it comes to something specifically related to the university, find out if others have had a similar problem organizing something then keyword search the issue and the college or school's name. You can also check forums and blogs to find out what others' experiences might have been. Include the issue then the keyword "forums" "blogs" and "reviews."

Life

It happens when life becomes so hectic that everything looks disorganized. Make your life easier by seeking the type of tools that can help you organize your life. Create a list of things that need to be organized from tasks during the day to upcoming holiday celebrations. Then include the desired way you would want the information to be delivered to you: forum, blog, video, article, radio, live chat, etc.

You can also subscribe to a website that provides you with useful tips to help you manage your life. Scroll the site for a subscribe button. In order to receive the latest information from the site, you will most likely need to register a user name, a first name, email address, and other details. Most websites are free to use. Do check terms and conditions by scrolling down the front page or clicking one of the tabs or links on the side of the page. Search "how to manage life" or "how to organize time" etc. My blog on organizing features people who enjoy creating ways to organize tools to parties, check out The Organizer (organizer-home.blogspot.com).

Getting your life organized is a topic that many speakers on YouTube, Blog Talk Radio and other places discuss. If you find you are having some difficulty getting started, check out motivational speakers who talk about whatever your concern. You can listen and watch many church services online if you feel you need to be addressing not only things like managing time, money and more, but spiritual issues as well.

Website Share

You can share files easily over the Internet. Elsewhere in this book I briefly mentioned about attaching large documents and being able to send them using additional services. The back up and file sharing services are beneficial when you are often producing material, have limited offline storage space, and need to get large files out to many people. You can keyword search "file sharing and back up."

Now let's say you don't want to just share media, but you want to collaborate about it with others. Maybe a co-worker wants to add something to it and someone else needs to edit the work. File-sharing tools are available online. You can keyword search "top file-sharing tools" and include the keyword "collaboration."

So what if you want to share a link, video, audio, or something else with someone? Sharing links are quite easy because there are usually icons of popular social media websites somewhere to the side or at the bottom of the website. If you click on one of your favorite sites like Facebook or Google Plus to share images and documents with your friends, you will be able to simply log in and make your link available to your network. But if there are no visible ways to share a link then use the traditional method which is to copy the link in the address bar and then paste it wherever you want. Since many links are very long, there are sites that will shorten your links so that they are easy to send via your micro-blogging sites where characters are limited as well as other places. Keyword search: "how to shorten links."

Now if you have a website or blog, you would like to make sharing links available to your audience, there are share buttons. To get the sharing tool for your site, keyword search "share buttons for website." If you would like for me to share your link on one of many blogs and other sites, do contact me. I have thousands of viewers who visit various sites. Join one of my Twitter sites www.twitter.com/cashbusinessnow for those interested in making additional money.

4 Computers

When I first sat in front of the computer I was about nine years old in the fourth grade. The school year was 1985-86. Back then, I had an African American teacher named Mrs. Middleton who was a computer whiz. She taught my friends and I basic computer programming. We had Apple Basic Computer Programming workbooks next to our keyboards open and always ready to follow instructions. There weren't many computers in the lab, because the keyboards, the monitors and the hard drives were all big, sturdy, and took up much space.

I was amazed and bored at the same time looking at the neon green letters and numbers on the computer screen. I thought the keyboards were far better than the typewriters I had at home. I also found it quite interesting that with a series of letters, signs and numbers I could make all sorts of cool things show up on the screen. One image I remembered creating was Christmas tree, that wasn't a clipart image or photo, but just a series of Xs and Os I inputted that showed up on the screen in a pyramid shape. Through a series of codes it formed the design.

By the time I reached middle school in 1987, I couldn't believe how DOS, the operating system I once worked with was an option and that Microsoft Windows had come along and turned the way we all viewed the computer upside down! I still hadn't seen the full color version at the time, but was happy for the miniature looking MAC computer that displayed some easy to use software. I was surprised that all one had to do was just double click to open a program, stretch boxes, move them out the way or scroll down to view--this was so amazing to me at the time.

For years, I recreated the same eye-opening experiences all over again when I began searching for the latest, best, great, and the top ten computers, software programs, accessories and more annually for a time.

So why not find out what does the technological world have to offer today to excite you? What might you be missing out on?

Internet Services

I have far too many stories about how the Internet has been integral in my life. It has definitely helped me in so many ways from finding medical information to helping me obtain a job. Now when it comes to having the Internet on your computer, you definitely want to have some options when it comes to accessing it. You don't have to stick with the Internet service that was provided for you by default when you bought your computer.

Look for other "Internet services." Notice the features they offer and then download a couple of choices. This way if you have trouble accessing one, you have others or maybe you want different servers open at the same time.   There are some good online browsers that are specifically designed for children to use as well as those with special needs, and more. You can also check offline to see what is available at your local office supplies store.

Hardware

When it comes to computer hardware issues, you will need to have your model name; serial information and any other details that will help you diagnose what the trouble might be. Oftentimes people have difficulty with their devices and simply do not know where to begin. Jot down what is happening with the equipment, then use your search engine to find out if others are having similar problems.

Software

There are numerous sites that have software for just about any issue. You will want to be careful not to download yet another problem, so seek sites that are highly rated, and don't have many ads and pop ups. Also uncheck those small boxes that want you to download additional software.

Whatever your software need, chances are a company has created something to solve your issue. Also, consider watching video and reading about new classes that are currently available. There are many certification courses online that will help you obtain additional knowledge in technology. Use keywords like: "free computer courses," "certified training in computer," and "computer classes for credit" to get you started.

Graphics

Since there are a variety of ways to view graphics, you will need to take a moment to search what your preference is or concern and then follow instructions. I recall a time when my graphics on my computer were doing some strange things. Images via the Inter-net were no longer coming up even after a few upgrades. I learned that not only was my computer outdated, but that there was also something happening with my video card. Needless to say, I had to get rid of the computer. The information superhighway was simply too fast for it!

Common Computer Issues

I have unfortunately dealt with most of the following issues, so if you recognize one on this list, start performing your searches and include the keyword "videos." Chances are you will be able to fix it without a professional if you are pretty computer savvy.

1. Malicious software includes: viruses, spyware, adware, trojan horses, worms, rootkits, and other things that are created to hurt your computer. Usually if you have these issues, you will not only delete cookies and do other routine maintenance, but it is a must that you download software that handles not only viruses but malware too. Find out what products are highly rated and then choose one to download.

2. Slow computer was a common one with most people I know. Oftentimes people just save things to their computers and never bother to clean them. They download all sorts of items with advertising attached. They also let others use their computer only to discover that a certain file or program is so large it is eating up space. So when this happens, you will need to start deleting what you don't need, remove cookies (the tracking tools left behind from visiting Internet websites), transfer data to storage devices and perform a full scan on your computer.

3. Internet or network connectivity problems such as you were able to access the Internet on one day, but not today. You will need to unplug the modem(s) or hit the restart button(s). You might also need to contact the company that provides your Internet service.

4. Environment issues. From cigarette smoking to the room being too hot, computers will go haywire from dust, static electricity, drastic temperature changes, etc.

5. Hard drive failure. Your computer no longer turns on or does other things that affect its performance. This is never a good sign and if a system reboot doesn't work, it is safe to say you just might need to purchase a new hard drive or computer, but before you do, check with a professional.

6. Dead power supply. This occurs when your computer was just working the other day, but when you go to power it on, nothing happens because it was unplugged from the wall or the outlet no longer works. If all was checked and still a problem, contact a professional.

7. Missing CD/DVD Drive. You were playing a movie or CD, but then when you attempt to use your drive again the computer acts as if it isn't there. You will need to know your operating system and then search on the Internet for instructions on how to get the software to work again. If all appears well and still doesn't work, you may have problems with your drive.

8. Blue screen of death. This is an error screen that shows up after a fatal system error with the Windows computer system. An issue like this requires a professional if you don't have the patience and time to restore your computer to the manufacturer settings.

9. Black screen in windows will not boot in safe mode or any other mode. Seek professional advice it might be a simple fix, but then maybe not.

10. Slow or lagging performance. You can free up the storage space on your hard drive and increase the speed with periodic maintenance. Type in search engine "how to clean hard drive," "how to increase computer speed" or "how to free up space on hard drive" Other times this happens due to a recent change on your computer, downloading a software program, a virus has found its way in the system, or some other reason. If you don't

know what might be the problem, it is always best to go with a professional. Keyword search: "computer repair" and add your city and state in the browser.

Security

With so much identity theft and other related issues, you can never be too safe when browsing online. There are many programs that help children browse and others that protect your information on your computer, website passwords, and more. Look up the latest computer security programs, systems, inventions, etc. to see what you might need.

Systems

When conducting a general search for the keywords: computer systems, you will need to narrow your search. What types of computer systems? Are you seeking the latest trending computer equipment? Do you need a list of computer systems? Is there a specific computer operating system you are inquiring about? Maybe you are in search of computer hardware. As you can see, sometimes if there is no specific search conducted you can confuse yourself and overwhelm others.

Computer Shopping

Browsing the web for a new computer doesn't have to be a challenge. There are plenty of consumer reports that can help you reach a good decision. Before you buy your next computer, consider what you will be doing with it each day. Does it have to be portable, stationary, used for gaming, etc.? If the computer's speed, a large, expandable hard drive, a touch screen, and other features are necessary, then you would look for items that have your top preferences. For example, you can begin a general search by putting in keywords: "buy computer with fast hard drive" and then include your desired price. Visit a price comparison website once you have a brand and type in mind to get a good deal and also don't forget checking for sites that offer coupons and/or discounts to shop.

Since the features on computers and other similar devices are often changing, perform research on what might be suitable for your needs. Pay attention to memory, speed, and other specifications to make sure you are choosing a device that can handle your tasks. Most laptops that are inexpensive only provide the basics like web browsing and word processing. According to Square Trade research nearly one in three laptops fail over three years.

5 Shopping

When it comes to shopping online you will need to have a note pad, pen, and your credit card or a debit card with a limit handy. Some things to keep in mind if you are the buyer, you will need to be aware of where a business is located, what people are saying about it, and how you can save money on your purchases. Now if you are a seller, you have to be concerned about meeting the needs of your customers, taking great care to deliver quality products and services, and competitive pricing so that shoppers can keep coming back to your store. There is no best way to shop that fits all personalities, but what we can all agree on when it comes to online shopping and selling on websites is seek out merchants that save consumers' time, money and offer quality services and products.

Classifieds Ads

This is a simple way to advertise all those items you have lay-ing around the house you no longer use as well as buy used ones for reasonable prices. There are many different types of classified ad websites to research. The best ones are those in your local area that are popular. With more visitors, the chances you will sell an item are quite good. You can check them out by putting in the name of your city and include the word "classifieds."

You will see a list of websites showing ads in your area. Now some are paid classified ad services and others are for free. If you want to post items to sell, but don't want to pay for advertising then search for the websites that host "free classifieds." However, keep in mind that your results may not be that good on some sites.

When visiting classifieds, you will need to do the following: register, create a user name and password. You will also need to type in your ad and upload a photo (if necessary) to the site. You may be asked to include a phone number, an email address which you will be given the option to make it public. Some of the popular websites do have fees depending on what you are selling, so have your credit card handy. Be sure you check reviews before keying in your information.

Uploading photos

If you don't know how to upload a photo, there are sites that will provide you with video instructions on how to do it. Simply type in your search engine the phrase, "how to upload photos from computer to web page."

If you have no clue how to take quality pictures of your merchandise, do check out what others have done. Search for ads that are similar to what you are selling. You can also search "how to take photos of..." include what it is you would like to photograph.

Here are some ideas for using classifieds besides selling items:

- Local events
- Real Estate
- Free information
- Contests
- Obituaries
- Birth announcements
- Classes
- Coupons

When people shop offline rarely do they think about the savings they might get on name brand items especially if they are on sale. You can save a lot of money if you just listed the brand name items and then placed that list next to the computer and started searching for coupons for each. You can do this by including the company name and then adding "printable coupons" or be specific and add the year and the kind of coupons you are interested in such as: grocery coupons, manufacturer coupons, and restaurant coupons.

Coupon Codes

Don't forget when shopping online, look for store coupon codes. These are used to help you save money on your online orders. There are boxes usually available somewhere near the end of your order. You will type whatever coupon code is offered by a store into the boxes provided. They are usually brief letters with a number or some odd phrase. Typically only one coupon code is accepted per purchase, but sometimes websites might accept more than one.

Just a reminder, you will want to save some money when you shop online. You can check out some coupon codes for major retail and online stores at a site called, RetailMeNot. In addition, you can conduct a web search and include the store name and the words "coupon codes." You will find additional sites that will list new as well as old coupon codes.

Coupon Toolbars and Tracking

There are many coupon websites. Some will want you to download toolbars to your computer before they will allow you to print coupons from their sites. Others will ask that you register and then you can navigate through the sites for what you want.

You might see companies who offer memberships to coupon sites and then they might prompt you to download a coupon toolbar. Once you become a member, you will get access to all sorts of coupons. Don't be deceived, it shouldn't cost you anything to use these online services, but time. Also, beware of pop up ads and other annoying things that show up when visiting these sites.

Many stores will save cookies on your computer. Basically what this means is that they will track what websites you are visiting and send advertising based on what you just looked at to their servers. You might think it is a bit strange you just visited a site and now you see their ad on just about every site you visit. Don't think for one minute it must be a divine act of God that an ad displayed on the right side of your computer with something similar to what you just looked at—the cookie did it. You can remove cookies off your computer. So how might you do that? Search "how to get rid of cookies video." There is plenty of video tutorials explaining what to do.

Also, keep in mind the stores that you enjoy shopping sometimes have online coupons you can obtain at their sites. So visit the store site by name to find out what you have been missing and register at your favorite store websites. Join the email list if you should want to keep up-to-date with the latest store specials.

Coupon Apps

There are a variety of services that will help you save money when you choose to download their apps to your portable electronic devices. You can also search "smart coupons" or "mobile coupons." Find out what incentives your favorite stores are offering if you should include them on your phone.

Offline Coupons

Don't sleep on those fliers and envelopes that come through your mail. Many of them advertise websites that offer savings if you should order items online. Look for coupon codes and compare your savings if you should shop online or offline.

Also, keep in mind the numerous loyalty programs and apps that can help you save even more money. Take some time to look up websites that offer discounts, coupon codes, rebates, and e-bates when you shop.

I created an e-book to help shoppers seek deals year round not just during Black Friday and Cyber Monday. Consider the money-saving tips for online and offline shopping in my informative guide, *Black Friday, Cyber Monday Strategies to Use Year Round* by Nicholl McGuire.

Ecommerce and Online Banking

Paying people with cash or check is a thing of the past thanks to online payment websites like PayPal. If you need to pay someone or get paid, then that email address you created will come in handy. The person says, "I'm sorry I don't have any cash on me," then you say, "No problem, I accept credit cards." They will be shocked, "You do?"

Whether you swipe with a device attached to your mobile device, scan a check or know of other ways (search: new ways to accept payments). Also, visit PayPal, Dwolla or a similar online payment site that accepts funds from individuals. The person will put in his or her credit card information into the safe and secure website and then pay you like they would if they were paying a bill online. The site asks the customer for your email address and then before long, you will be receiving an email saying something like, "You have cash…" It's that simple!

You can also request debit cards from these e-commerce (electronic payment) sites. They operate just like the ones at your bank. The difference between the bank and the ecommerce site, you will be charged a fee if you use them at an ATM. The online payment site will also deduct a small fee (pennies on the dollar) for things like eBay transactions. So search for "ecommerce sites" or "online payment websites" to see most recent. Register with the site. You will need to have a bank account to validate your account. You will also provide basic information just like you would if you were opening up a bank account minus the ID.

Online banking and ecommerce sites are great for people who need to track spending better, those that may not trust a relative with their offline banking card, or just want to set up an account to use specifically for Internet purchases.

Online Banking

One of the most convenient and useful services on the Internet is indeed online banking! It eliminates the need to visit a bank, sit on the phone, or write out checks. Simply go online, log into your account and perform all your business transactions on your bank's secure website.

The first thing you will want to do is visit the bank's site. You will see an option to register and begin your online banking. However, if you find it overwhelming, see an offline banking representative who will walk you through the process. There are also online video tutorials that will show you how simple it is to register for an online banking account.

Electronics

Many electronics go on sale during the holidays. What you might find is there are a lot of websites that will offer cheap versions of all sorts of electronics to lure customers into their stores. Mean-while, the better versions of the gadgets haven't changed much in price. When shopping for electronics, be sure to check the store's refund policies, warranties, and any additional information that can help you just in case something goes wrong with the product.

Since there are far too many websites that sell electronics, I will not list them here, but I will suggest the following when researching an item:

1. Search for your desired product by using the brand and model name if you have it.

2. Perform keyword searches based on what kind of device it is followed by a few words that might describe its function.

3. Place the name of the product and how much you are willing to pay for it.

4. Find out what others are saying about it on social media sites, forums, and product review sites.

5. Post a question about the product and see what comes up in the search engines.

6. If you can't find it online, call a local store to see if they might carry it or know of a supplier who has it.

7. Watch videos on a video sharing site about the item.

8. Check an online auction site to see how the gadget looks/operates once it becomes older.

9. Find out more about the product by checking out Google or Bing images.

10. Check out price comparison shopping sites.

Remember if you have never shopped with a website, do find out where it is located, check for contact information, and the Better Business Bureau or find out if there are online reviews about it. Call the website or send an email to see if customer service is still active. Note how long it takes for them to respond to your inquiry if at all.

Food

How can the Internet best be used when it comes to something like food? Well there are many ways that people have used the Internet to meet needs. The following list is just a start of the endless possibilities you can enhance your taste buds while making your body look and feel healthy.

1. Look up recipes based on interests, health concerns, budget, etc.
2. Check ingredients in foods you buy.
3. Save on items by downloading and printing coupons.
4. Buy items online in bulk.
5. Discover new ways to enhance food.
6. Find out latest food products created.
7. Learn how foods are made.
8. Take healthy food quizzes.
9. Watch food preparation shows.
10. Upload family recipes and make money with them at certain websites.
11. Find out new stores in the area.
12. Discover food events coming to the area.
13. Upload photographs of favorite foods on social networking sites or share links.
14. Test recipes in forums and get feedback.

15. Create recipe books.

16. Meet people who like the same foods you like via online dating websites, forums, clubs, social networking, and more.

17. Enter food related sweepstakes.

18. Have samples sent to your home.

19. Participate in online diet programs.

20. Talk with a dietician online who can create a meal plan program customized for you.

21. Set up offline meet and greets based on food interests.

23. Join a service that delivers food to your doorstep.

24. Learn how to use food to decorate a table, create sculptures, and do other creative things.

25. Find out the calories of certain foods you eat.

26. Get discounts to local restaurants.

27. Invite relatives and friends to web pages related to food.

28. Collaborate on online food projects using Google documents.

29. Vent about foods and restaurants through review sites.

30. Create an online business plan for food related business.

31. Learn how to invent your own product.

32. Attend an online seminar or webinar about food industry.

33. Visit websites of celebrities who are considered master chefs.

34. Announce your events using press releases, classified ads, email, social networking, etc.

35. Research culinary schools.

36. Learn more about food via online classes.

37. Discover the history about certain foods.

38. Search for nearby wineries and visit.

39. Learn about what certain cultures enjoy eating.

40. Find out about current and old foods you once ate and their origins.

41. Redefine your mother or grandmother's old recipes so that you are eating healthy.

42. Learn about portion control when eating and when is the best time to stop eating.

43. Discover what snacks and drinks are considered un-healthy.

44. How to make your own salad dressings, sauces and gra-vies.

45. How to make your own desserts.

46. How to create certain foods like popular restaurants. (An excellent way to save money!)

47. Create an infograph (a visual online poster with charts and other graphics) to help cooks, introduce new foods, or encourage healthy eating.

You just received a lot of things you can use the Internet for when it comes to food related research. All the best to you! And while you're at it, you might want to learn about new ways to exercise and what herbal remedies, vitamins, cell salts, and prescription medicines are beneficial to you and which ones aren't. You will be reminded again in this book to perform some health related research.

Freebies

I have had my share of freebies sent to my home after filling out online forms, surveys, and specifically searching for items. Retail websites sometimes offer free items and not everything is a scam or useless. One of the best items I received for free after participating in a study was a Microsoft webcam. So how do you go about getting free items? Well, every site you shop on, always check to see if they have a mailing list or something similar that provides giveaways and then register. This way you will receive offers. Now let's get on with the searching.

Perform a general search for "freebies" and you will see websites advertising free stuff, samples, and you might even find some that mention "real freebies." I would start with those first. Most sites do mention shipping and handling charges.

Next, narrow your search to a specific need. Maybe you hope to land a free item that costs thousands, right? Unfortunately many of those websites want you to join numerous businesses, spend much money, take surveys, and do other things before you are even eligible to enter the sweepstakes. I learned the hard way searching "free computer" such a waste of time and money. However, who knows, you might find a free electronic or something else worthwhile if you check the online classifieds.

Continue to search for more freebies. Maybe you would like free things like: food, cosmetics, feminine products, health items, household stuff, baby things, books, magazines, pet products, office supplies, and more. There are many more sites that offer coupons, deals, deep discounts, buy one get one free, and rebates for all of these things, so add the specific items in your research and include those keywords too.

When you decide on what sites you would like to register with, don't use your main email. Instead, use a different one so that your inbox will not be flooded with a bunch of useless mail. Also, it isn't necessary to supply a phone number, but most sites will require a mailing address if you want items sent to your residence. For a long time now, Walmart offers freebies. Keyword search: Walmart Freebies.

Other search terms you might want to use include: top freebie sites, freebies by mail without surveys, best freebie sites and best sites for free stuff. Don't forget to include any specific requests.

Gifts

When you just don't have much time or money, there are many ways on the Internet to show loved ones you care. Take a moment to think about those "thinking of you" gifts. You can send a beautiful photo, clipart or artwork online to someone's email. Search for "online cards" or "flowers by email" to get started.

Consider sending a free audio-book or music to a friend, a favorite television show clip to a relative, or send a secret crush note to someone. You can make a slideshow with a loved one's favorite images too and add music. All of these tips are searchable, start with "how to" or "sites with" then simply put in various related keyword phrases and scroll down the list until you find a site worth checking out.

Gift Ideas

Sometimes you have the money to spend, but you just don't know what to spend it on. Knowing the person's interests will help you select a memorable gift. Type the person's interest and include "gift ideas" or look up gifts for specific people "gift ideas for..." i.e.) gift ideas for men, gift ideas for mom, gift ideas for teachers. You can also search "unique gift ideas" to find appealing sites.

Online Shopping Tips

From sites that give things away to those who have a deal of a day like Woot, you can find some fun ways to shop online. Type "deal of the day" add a product name. Next, start surfing various web-sites to see what some have to offer. Never shop stores again without stopping at sites first that offer discounts, coupons and rebates. You can save money this way. Also, don't pay full price for any product without searching a "comparison shopping" web-site first. Google has a site called, Froogle, that can help you with this, but also check other similar sites as well. Sometimes web-sites will favor certain stores over others, so be sure you are checking other sources. You will be able to find the lowest price to pay for an item by reviewing store prices all on one page.

Don't sleep on online yard sales via classified advertisements, auction sites and other places people use to buy and sell their goods. As indicated in the classified ad section previously, there are plenty of apps that help sellers connect with local buyers.

Shopping Tools

There are many shopping tools that can assist you with finding unique and fun items. You can visit a site like FindGift. You can also track and watch the price history of a product using Camel-CamelCamel. Finally, there is Craiglook that makes it easy to browse Craigslist. Inventors are always looking for ways to enhance an existing website so search the name of the website you commonly buy items and then add the keyword "tools" to find out the latest inventions.

Since the Internet is forever evolving and many sites in this book may one day be no more or names might change, you will want to search out what your specific needs might be and then take a look at new websites. For instance, let's say you are interested in learning more about the newest shopping websites and tools for something in particular; you would search "top comparison shopping sites" or "shopping websites reviews" + your item.

Scams

Whenever you are shopping online and discover a new website to buy from, do take a moment to check the Better Business Bureau and consumer review sites like Yelp. You can also put in the name of the company and include the words "rip off" and "scam." Get tips on how to have a hassle-free online shopping experience simply by putting in search terms like "shopping online safety tips" or "latest website scams."

Personal Style

Have you ever considered allowing the Internet to give you a fashion make-over? Well there are many websites that do just that. From your hairstyle to the shoes you wear, some sites will allow you to upload a photo of yourself. You are then able to see what your head looks like with or without hair. You can choose various hairstyles and colors.

When it comes to shopping for clothes and shoes, you can actually dress yourself up or others online. Some offline stores have a web camera available on site for you to stand in front to see how a dress might look without having to go in the dressing room to try it on. You can pair items online before you buy them from some websites. Look for those with these features the next time you shop online.

If you don't like what is available on some sites, you can design your own apparel. Simply search "design your own…" and include what it is you might want to customize. Maybe there is a hat, shoes, purse, wallet, or other item you would love to make your own.

Would you like to see closely some clothing online? Well there are many websites that let you zoom in on the fabric at various angles. When you visit a site, take a moment to click on the image or hover over it. Check to see if you are able to enlarge it. Also, notice small images of the same item below the photograph. The view features are especially handy when it comes to electronics. You might need to know what outputs are available on the side or the back of a device before purchasing it.

Always scroll to the bottom of the web page to see what customers say about the product, check ratings on the site, but also compare with others. It is unfortunate, but some companies do pay writers to create reviews.

Price Comparisons

This was the best tool web developers could have come up with for those of us who like to visit comparison shopping sites. These websites eliminate the need to drive up and down the street and across town looking for the best prices on something for the household. You simply search for "comparison shopping" then include what you are looking for. You will find sites that will direct you to the product you are seeking while you observe a list of prices that best suit your budget.

When there are many websites to view, you can filter the list by searching: price, product, style or whatever else the website will allow you to search. However, sometimes what you see on some comparison shopping sites isn't always what you think you might get. Perform further research and you just might find the product cheaper elsewhere. Always begin your search with your favorite store then use comparison shopping web pages to find the best quality and affordable prices.

Shopping Review Sites

The great thing about shopping review sites, they keep you from impulsive spending if you take the time to read comments and compare your desired product to recommendations. For instance, let's say I would like to purchase a new stove. I wouldn't immediately go to the nearest store and be greeted by a salesperson who would direct me to something I might like. Instead, I would search the Internet for what might be important to me. First, I would check the color of a stove, next the features, and of course cost. I would then include specifically what I wanted in the search engine. "Black stove, four burners, self-cleaning" and then check the price.

Now you might include a price range between whatever you could afford and a specific price. Then you would visit the recommended sites. Select maybe two or three top choices. Next, go to a search engine and include the model name along with comparison shopping sites to see what other merchants are selling it for. Finally, you would print out the web page that meets your needs then head over to the store. By doing this, some store representatives will either meet or beat the price on the paper you brought to them. Far too many people still don't use this effective method of shopping before they buy.

What more can I say about online comparison shopping? It's easy. Once you get the hang and habit of doing it, you will always think, "Let me check the Internet before I go spending my money on something I might not like or need." You will find yourself seated in front of the computer doing things like: seeking coupons, opening several different websites and toggling between them. In addition, reading product reviews, not just on one site but others. I would also suggest view video websites to see how the products you like work before you go out and buy. The store representative will just love you for it. The less time he or she has to spend selling you on a product, the better-- he or she wants to move on to more customers and more sales! You want to get on with your day too.

From food to tools, you can compare price, quality, ease of use, features, and more using a variety of websites. There are also online quizzes at some sites that will help you make a good decision. For instance, if you think you might need a certain tool for a task, you would put the name of the tool in the search engine and include the word "ideas" or "uses" and then see how others might use it. You could also include words like "quizzes," "questionnaires" or "surveys" to see if a company is collecting data from consumers about the tool.

Shopping can be quite entertaining and helpful both on and off-line if you are patient when it comes to searching and browsing. The Internet isn't perfect, but it can be an integral asset in your life when you make the most of it!

6 Internet Safety

After spending much time on the Internet, you will eventually run into websites that carry their share of viruses. Further, you will find windows prompting you to download many things. With so many strange things going on, you might not want to use the Internet for awhile or go on certain websites, but don't fear. Those feelings will pass and you will be ready to start searching again. Be sure your computer is equipped with virus protection and other software specifically created to keep you from being tempted to click on risky pop up ads and other similar things.

Tips on Visiting Unfamiliar Websites

Over the years, the Internet has been a huge blessing in my life. It is because of this very beneficial tool that I have been able to do things like: save money, make money, find lost friends, obtain instructions for various electronic equipment, avoid potential problem people, places, and things and a host of other activities too numerous to count.

Before I do anything on any website, I am looking for two things: something about the company, frequently asked questions, and where to register. Depending on the service needed, I will view the company's 'Terms and Conditions.'

Website Reviews

I check to see what other visitors' experiences have been like with a website before I register or make a purchase. By taking just a few minutes to scroll through the reviews, I learn whether a site is worth signing up. I also find what potential issues might be if I have selected a product for purchase on the site such as how difficult it might be to build or use. Sometimes product reviews can be nothing more than smoke and mirrors, because some companies will pay people to write good reviews about them. Visit various sites with comment sections rather than just one to make an informed decision.

Rip-offs, Complaints

If there are many complaints such as: customer service issues, frequent website problems, and other negative issues, I don't join/buy from the site. You can find out more about any website simply by including keywords in your search like: scam, rip off, complaints, Better Business Bureau (BBB), and other similar words. Your local BBB comes in handy if something should arise regarding your online purchase. I usually contact the company directly before escalating the situation.

Although most home pages of websites are attractive, organized, and easy to operate, there are also many that are nothing more than false storefronts. Even if you do take the time to view some sites carefully, there is always the possibility of a potential challenge, so be cautious when opening email, sharing information, making purchases, and registering on websites.

Privacy & Protection

You can find the latest information about scam sites by visiting the Federal Trade Commission website (consumer information) and contacting them about your experiences. You can check to see if a website is infected by using "free online security services." You can keyword search "report scam websites" to find additional places where you can post your thoughts. A site that I have found useful over the years has been Ripoffreport.com. You can find comparable sites simply by searching "frauds" and "scams" and including the keyword "forums".

Remember to keep the following in mind when visiting sites:

1. Search the company name and include words like fraud, scam, rip off, and complaints.

2. Do check the company name with the BBB.

3. Find out if others have shopped on the site by visiting forums that discuss fraudulent activities and searching the company name within the site. Sometimes the businesses will not come up in the main search engines, so you have to do some digging.

4. Some businesses operate under other names. So keep your eye out for similar companies, websites, business owners, etc.

5. Don't provide any information, make purchases, or refer the company to others until you are comfortable and have had an enjoyable experience.

6. Be sure you have read the 'About Us' section, noted contact information, and checked out refund/exchange policies before buying.

7. Notice whether the site is official. Many websites will have some kind of indication in the address bar like an icon of a lock or a color code to indicate that the site is legitimate. If you don't see any indication that the site is official, search again and watch for misleading advertisements.

7 Finances

When it comes to finances, you can get a lot done online. You may already use banking online, but what if you would like to do more? How about signing up for a new checking or savings account online? Maybe you would like to start investing? How about seeking new ways to manage or make money? Well, whatever your interest, this list might generate some more ways to use the Internet to watch your money grow.

Accounting Software

Whether you have a small business or you are a highly organized individual that would prefer to keep track of your finances using accounting software, there are some good ones out there, but they aren't cheap. One of the first things you will want to do is check reviews and "compare accounting software." Once you click on a site to help you with your purchase, you should be able to read reviews, visit the website, and compare features.

Rates

Finding the current interest rates is simple. But when visiting a site, notice if it is reputable. Some of the best ones provide interactive tools. You can ask the service what you are looking for by typing in your request. The latest rate information is usually on the front page of the company website or a link to another web page might be provided. A one-stop rate website will give you recent mortgage, refinance, auto, CDs, checking and savings information. Just put in the search engine what specific rates you are looking for (i.e. bank rates) or use a general term like "rates."

Stocks

Stock trading, trading tools, and the present condition of the stock market will typically show up when you search "stocks." If you are interested in learning more about the stock market, consider watching a video on your favorite video sharing site and use the keyword search term: "how to invest in stocks" or read a how-to article or book.

Financial Investment Companies

If you should want to do some major financial planning for your future or desire to invest inherited wealth, lottery winnings and other financial windfalls of money, then you will want to learn more about "financial advisors" or "financial planner." You can also search "insurance companies" to find out recent information to help you make an informed decision.

Take a moment to research well-known investment companies and if you don't there are plenty of suggested lists. You might even notice that in the Google search engine, your location is tracked and recommendations in your area will show up. I would personally begin my search with local companies. We are talking about your money, so it would make sense to deal with an organization you can drive or walk to, but also has a stellar reputation. Once you have made your selection, search for reviews about that company. Keep in mind, businesses pay well to have a good online reputation so do some digging and interview people offline about the financial consulting office you have chosen.

Cash Conversion

You might want to know what certain foreign currency is worth. You can do this by searching for a "currency converter" and also check "cash conversion live rates." You can learn more about "cash conversion cycle" which is one of several ways a company measures how fast it can convert cash on hand into more cash, according to Investopedia.

Savings Bonds

When you want to learn more about savings bonds such as: how to make a purchase, calculate the value of your paper saving bonds, or transfer funds to your bank account, you can go to TreasuryDirect.gov.

Salaries

See section on employment.

Taxes

Annually people pay taxes and so the government is always looking for ways to make it easy for them to get paid. There are more than enough websites about taxes. Anything you want to know about the IRS is on the Internet--good, bad and ugly. You will find tax software available online or it can be downloaded to your computer. Tax preparation offices will show up in the search engine within your local area.

You can find out about ways to save money, make a payment, and get the current forms and publications on the Irs.gov website. In addition, there are videos, articles, blogs, reports, presentations, and more to help students, retirees, independent contractors, business owners, and others pay taxes. So when a specific issue comes up regarding your taxes, type the question in the search engine. After conducting a search, you will find sites with professionals ready to answer your questions via live chat for free or for a small fee.

Law

Knowing the local laws in your area isn't a bad thing to do especially when you have recently relocated. Why not conduct a search with the name of the community you reside and include the law that you are curious about? For instance, I once worked in Pasadena CA so I included "laws" and then found some information about nuisance violations. You might be interested in local laws and how they relate to you.

Fun Finance Stuff

A couple of things that might be fun for you are to keyword search: "find money" "need money" and "how much is (type in the name of a collectible) worth." Randomly putting information about your finances isn't a waste of time, that's how you find some interesting websites and soon you will have many favorites. Be sure to use your bookmark tool as you find useful sites.

Now when it comes to saving money on and offline, consider visiting websites to help you with reducing expenses. After reading an article, I discovered that you can download apps that cost much less than buying a device like a GPS which assists with driving directions, detours and more. I also found buying any CDs, video games, and DVDs are such a waste when the Internet has so many businesses that offer music and movie subscriptions.

What else might you be able to save money on? Well, you can start by using keyword searches like: "baby items waste of money" "power tool rentals" "toy rentals" "formal wear rentals" and "tips on saving money grocery shopping." Do check for the latest online tools to help you with your personal finances like "apps that save money to..." or "useful tips on saving (include your need).

The following is a list of more ideas. Notice that in order to get detailed information about a certain topic, you have to change how you search and spend a little more time thinking beyond the obvious keyword phrases about saving money.

1. how to save money on...You can include a specific need or consider these suggestions: groceries, electric bills, food, car insurance, gas, gas heat, cable, diapers, a wedding, etc.

2. top useless kitchen gadgets

3. cheapest (include the name of item)

4. best prices on (include name of item)

5. inventions that save us time

6. unnecessary costly pet products

7. top websites people like to shop for

8. affordable online shopping...You might include: for teens, colleges, apparel, etc.

9. business products save time

10. online tools saves time or tools to save money

11. cash generating opportunities (like becoming a lender rather than a borrower, how to sell certain items, ways bloggers and writers make money, etc.)

12. where to find cheap baby supplies (like formula, clothing, toys, etc.)

8 Research

Researching for pertinent information online is very easy to do, but what makes it challenging at times is when some websites have outdated articles, links that are inoperable, and sources that lack details. You may have figured out by now how to overcome some of these hurdles. Search engine companies are constantly making improvements. When it comes to searching for specific topics, try these tips:

1. Consider videos, slideshows, uploaded documents, and current documentaries about a subject when articles and other media can't be found or they cost much money to obtain. Filter your search by day, week, month or year.

2. Visit a library when you are overwhelmed with searching online. It can be less stressful sometimes when information is in your hand rather than seeking it over a screen. Keep in mind, there is still much literature, images, government records, family relics, reports, and more that is not available on the Internet and may never be. Talk with a librarian, an avid researcher or historian that may be able to help.

3. Check not-so popular websites and other alternative media that list many books, videos, and more for purchase and for free. You just might find that some Indie authors have good experiences that can help with the subject you are researching about.

4. Don't always believe what you have heard or read because an author, movie, or something else has been heavily promoted. Chances are there just might be an organization behind the work that is attempting to suffocate others who are telling the truth about something ongoing occurring in a certain industry.

5. Find out who has recently died or been jailed for a cause by including the industry name and words like "pioneer" "founder" "new discoveries" "whistleblower" "exposed" and "secrets."

6. You can curate content based on interests or organize it on a pin board like Pinterest and talk about your findings with others. You can also create an online newspaper or magazine with the content. Begin your search your way keyword search "create online newspapers" centered around your topic or "create online magazines" "create stories" "stumble sites"

You can create stories and timelines using Storify for readers to view. If you want to stumble sites based on your interests try StumbleUpon. When seeking the latest reports not provided by mainstream media keyword search your topic and include "alternative media." 7. You can preserve your research online using all sorts of social bookmarking sites, curating tools, and online storage which helps with compiling digital images, web links, and movie files making it also accessible to others for future use.

Some serious researchers will share that there is an Internet that is not available to the mainstream public. You can learn more about this as well. However, be advised that much of the material on underground websites is not censored and can be problematic if you don't know what you are doing. So consider the advice of those who dare to go where most people don't.

Health

Researching one's medical condition is so simple online. Making an appointment or chatting about your issue is also quite convenient as well.

Health Information

Basic health information is typically found on any fitness website, encyclopedia, or a timeless site like WebMd which has much health and medical news. It is considered one of the credible resources.

Fitness

You can learn about exercise programs and stay fit by watching online videos. Know your medical symptoms so that you are not participating in an activity that could inflame old injuries.

Nutrition

Meal plans are available online for any health condition. Numerous websites have downloadable forms you can hang on your refrigerator to help you stick with your eating schedule.

Health Questions

If you have health insurance, then most likely there is a website with possibly a nurse you can chat live with or call about an illness if you don't want to research your question online. But if you should want to use the Internet, be sure that the website is a trustworthy site and you might want to erase your history in case you don't want others to know about your health ailment. Cross reference what you have learned with other websites.

How To

As you know you can learn about anything on the Internet. There are popular websites like WikiHow that provide how-to information on relationships, hobbies, crafts, computers, and more. However, sometimes websites can be useless. Take for instance, the blogs, articles, and videos with outdated information that pop up after you search for a specific thing as mentioned earlier. I would proceed with caution when reading the work of someone who has not tried something, did very little research, didn't bother to interview others, or truly lived an experience.

You can usually tell that the article or video is general, lacks details or is insincere, because the publisher has no specific information, quotes from professionals, or personal knowledge of the subject. Further, you will notice when the information is no longer useful when industry related terms that were once used are no more. Always check at least three or four other references before beginning a do-it-yourself project or researching a subject and if it helps, include the current year in the search or if you are on a specific website conduct a filter search that targets the most recent posting.

Information Delivery

When searching for that thing you most want to do, have some idea whether you want to view the material online, print it out, watch it on video, download it in e-book form, listen via podcast, talk with someone live, order videos to watch offline, or obtain media via email, etc.

Searching

Always narrow your search. You can do this by including more specific keywords. For instance, if I want to learn "how to paint" I know I am going to find all sorts of subjects about painting. But if I specifically type "how to paint a wall," I am going to get some information that is more centered on what I want. But that might not be good enough so I would add "how to paint a bedroom wall using semi-gloss paint." I could make the search even more specific by including the brand name and the size of the wall. The more specific you are when it comes to any "how to" subject, the less time you spend online looking at material that has nothing to do with what you really want.

Media Reporting

One of the best ways to enhance your critical thinking skills online is to read news that challenges your mind, body and spirit to think more deeply--the kind of information that will cause you to question, "Why?" You might be a working parent, a student in school, a mother unemployed, a man in jail, a senior retired, or a person with many health ailments, but what you are not is some-one incapable of questioning the world around you.

So why not ask the 5 Ws and the H when it comes to the news that is being broadcasted on the front pages of your favorite websites. There is always a reason why some news, editorials and feature stories are heavily promoted and others not so much. If you noticed most newsworthy information that affects your daily living is typically near the bottom of popular search engine pages, found after clicking many links or is no where in view due to a broken link or a video is taken down.

You will see that as you look for more truthful, in-depth report-ing or check out alternative media, there will be those times where you will run into brick walls. The content may have been here today, but gone tomorrow. Sometimes the person who reported some eye-opening news will end up retracting statements, sud-denly become ill, deceased, or someone close to them and the research mysteriously dies. Compelling social media pages and person's online achievements may disappear or links become inoperable. Over time, the presence of whistleblowers' work gradually comes off the Internet, so if you don't create screenshots or download it. You might never see it again. Censoring will happen over time online by any elitist group who doesn't want the inquisitive public to know something.

I find that in order to get to the relevant information I want to know, I have to avoid all the celebrity news, eye-popping images, product ads, mute sound on videos, and ignore comedic features. Most local stories I will either perform an organic search and find the content or obtain offline media. I do this much when research- ing for a project or adding media to an informative blog I manage about celebrities, useful news, and more at: they- liewait.blogspot.com.

When watching television news on or offline, for the sake of time, you are not being given the whole story and are often left with more questions than answers. I find it disheartening to see how dumbed down our society is in so many ways due to govern- ment propaganda. Informative news to some is reduced to the weather, a favorite celebrity's actions, the latest car or some other invention, and the rise and fall of stock prices.

When quality news is presented, the public reaction can be so fickle. Many viewers and readers really could care less about so- called boring news, and don't bother to look for the story behind a major news story. What is really going on in our world? What is being covered up behind the scenes while what appears to be a newsworthy story is spreading like wildfire? Just scroll through the comment sections and you will find what some Internet surfers consider important while others will make a joke or flippant remark. Are celebrities really as important as mainstream networks make them out to be? Of course not! Yet, our society tunes into meaningless stories all the time while overlooking the meaningful ones. Do search for my book, *Now I See Truth* by Nicholl McGuire.

This unintelligence that many Americans have when it comes to what is essential news and what is not has been systematically promoted by those who are told by their bosses to give the public what they supposedly want. Big businesses don't want internal issues leaked. Celebrities don't want their real stories told. Government affiliates don't want their hands caught in any cookie jars. So reporters or eyewitnesses are not to tell the public certain things that will only lead to more questions.

Systems are put in place to protect those who want to be protected even on the Internet. Webmasters and owners are paid well to ensure that some stories, legal documents, video and other things never reach the eyes of the curious public. Society's mindset is changed/rearranged/controlled by powerful entities so that there are no massive protests on or offline that might go against anything that would cause government, big businesses, secret groups, and celebrity teams to stop certain practices, make some changes, and do what is in the best interest of the people. One thing is certain that as long as the slaves, poor, widows, stay-at-home parents, students, retirees, and dying are distracted there will be no uprising. I challenge you to dig a little deeper to find truth before you go along with believing heavily publicized manufactured stories and events.

When it comes to the humorous news, the frivolous things about people, places and things we have no connection to will continue to bombard various websites. There are good distractions when people are weary of bad news and want to escape their personal miseries. I dare some of you readers to make good use of your time on the Internet to find relevant news that makes you think and brings awareness to issues you may not have otherwise thought of. Change your routine a bit when it comes to reading news and search out some information about the people, places and things you favor and why you like them so much. Put a few questions about personal issues or professional woes and see what might come up.

Here's how you might begin unraveling a news story that you might be in doubt about:

1. Visit a site that you would consider a reputable news outlet.

2. Read a story that is not major news, but relevant to your life. For instance, let's say you read a story about unemployment. Rather than take what you have learned and believe it as fact, consider comparing the story with a similar one from the year before and the year before that one.

3. Now note patterns in what you have been told about a particular subject matter. Compare what you have read to "alternative media" sources. Allow your mind to ask questions such as: why did the unemployment rate rise this year, fall the next, and then fall again? What is impacting the decline? How does this affect the industry that I am in?

4. Now for purposes of this exercise, visit a site that posts companies that are laying people off. Notice any trends and see how they might relate to you or someone else's future.

5. After you have read more than one story related to you and your family and visited more than one media outlet including alternative media from sources that might have been former workers, try another exercise. Read a recent story about a famous person but someone you haven't seen in the media for awhile. Note the ones that often show up in the news (or the first pages of sites like Google). These are the puppets on strings that keep you

distracted so that you won't think about the leadership in your nation and what they are up to and also so that you won't get pass 10 pages or more to search for any eye-opening news. Ask yourself, "Why is this person considered so interesting at this time?" Chances are the individual is on the rise again (whether dead or alive) because a group that supports him or her stands to gain money for an upcoming project, business venture, newly found organization, or to promote an agenda (usually something that challenges traditional views i.e. men and young boys dressing and behaving like women.)

So the public relations team will work diligently to ensure that the "brand" is promoted heavily. The A-list or star celebrity is the front-runner for the product that is being promoted whether now or in the future. We can understand this when it comes to commercials, but these days reality shows on and off the Internet are big money-makers for businesses. People and products are strategically placed in the shows for marketing purposes. Dialogue between characters is included about the item to generate a buzz. Since you are conveniently watching the show on your computer or elsewhere, it is quite easy to open other windows, search for a product, make a purchase, send your friends a text, update your social networking page, post a blog entry, and then tweet about it in less than 10 minutes.

6. Now think about lifestyles for a moment. You grew up thinking a certain way about the choices people make, how they should and shouldn't live, and so on. Well there are many groups that push the moral compass in the way that they want it to go. What better way then to use the media to disrupt the public mindset in a gentle, non-threatening way. The social issues that were important to your grandparents and great grandparents were not neces-

sarily so if media programmed them to feel the way they wanted them to. The elders passed on to your parents how to feel about an issue based on the information given to them by mainstream media outlets. But what if someone stops the cycle and asks, "Why?" Unlike your ancestors, you can pick your own news and find enough information to help you come up with a reasonable approach as to why some issues are not important to you and your family and why others should be relevant.

The Internet is a great source when it comes to comparing facts, piecing together time lines, noticing repetitive patterns with many of these news stories. Although it can take much time, you will begin to see that during select times of the year holiday stories will be pushed to get you in the mood to shop. Other stories will come to the forefront to get you to invest and so on.

If a tragic event brought many views to a page, other sites will be sure to mention that same news story and similar ones for days and weeks. Almost like clock work, an organization will tell the media outlets to stop showcasing an event, a person, place or thing and then begin another story and another. If you don't choose your own media, it will be chosen for you. If you don't pick your own television shows, read books you enjoy, and visit sites you sincerely like, the business owners will push you in a direction they want you to go that will increase their online revenue. It is quite simple to do via Internet marketing with quality software programs, great social networking connections, and much more to get you to react.

Contrary to what we have all been fed for decades about what is newsworthy like: blood, guts, gore, celebrity, and sports is not all there is to living in America. Just like media programmed many of us to believe some things are important while other information not so much, we can change that by looking up what is valuable to our way of life. Pay attention when the disinformation agents are at work to keep you from investigating the stories you have been given. Use the Internet to sort out fact from fiction and if you can, using the same invention, seek out the people who were there on the frontline when the tragedy and other questionable events occurred like those who lived in the community when a situation happened, who read a bill before it was passed, worked at the company when a remarkable situation took place, and more. Find out what you can for yourself and avoid the hype!

People Search

A fun exercise to utilize your research skills would be to search your name. Put into the search engine window your name and see who or what comes up. The first ten pages may have some-thing about you. Then do the same thing for other relatives and friends. You can also find out where someone lives, how old they are, where they work, even how much they make annually. Some sites will reveal how much the property they live is worth and other sites will show the names of relatives connected with them. So if you ever wondered how did someone know that you and another person were related, it is very easy to do a people search even if they claim no one told them.

You can also learn more about people by searching "back-ground check websites." You can get full reports which include criminal background, property ownership, property liens, profes-sional licenses, social network affiliations, and other essential data. Also, relatives and neighbors might show up on some reports as well. None of the full service background checks are free. There are trials, but the information is very limited.

References

The Internet is not short on reference material to help with those cumbersome research projects. Whatever your topic, you can find things about it. Some online reference tools I like to use include: thesaurus, dictionary, rhyming dictionaries, quotes encyclopedias, geography, and local maps.

Let's say you are in need of a guide to help you with a writing task, a building project, or visual presentation, you can search your specific need and include "books" or "images" to see what comes up. Oftentimes people will take snippets of reputable sources and include the images in a slideshow and other places. Check the Fair Use Act to be sure you are handling the material lawfully.

Google has some great wall posters you can print or purchase to help with learning how to research. One poster mentions Google Scholar it helps you search and find relevant sources and get abstracts, conference papers and more. Keyword search for "recent articles", "related articles" and "cited by." In addition, Google has lesson plans for those interested in teaching others on how to improve their online searches.

Here are some interesting things you can research online:

1. A specific country's flag and its origin.

2. Famous people from the 18th century who designed architecture.

3. Popular quotes taken from United States Presidents about money.

4. Best inventions of all time that made preparing food easier.

5. Innovative technological inventions from the previous year in the automotive industry.

6. Cool products that help infants go to sleep.

7. Strange people who live in undeveloped land in North America.

8. A comparison study between two ethnicities or two religious faiths.

9. A political movement that started protests around the world.

10. A town or city that was once thriving, but is now abandoned.

Organizing Research

When it comes to researching one or many topics at once, you will definitely need computer equipment that can handle all of those tabs you open. Seeking useful material is a cinch as you already know. There are many ways to research, but choosing how you want that information delivered and the way you want it stored can be a challenge especially when there isn't a lot of quality material about a specific subject.

One of the best ways to organize your information you find is through social bookmarks. By choosing a site that lets you collect various website links online, you are able to access the data from any computer. These social bookmarking sites are great when you don't want to store all the links on your hard drive. Many of these sites have useful sorting features as well. You can name them, assign tags or labels for easy reference, and star them.

If you would like to highlight or circle your online findings, there are Internet tools that you can use, check add-ons which are typically provided with your Internet service provider. Type the name of the company and then include the keyword "add-ons" to see what is available. Also, take advantage of online tools that help with spelling and grammar.

Another option when organizing research is to open a word processing software program on your computer. Type or copy and paste website addresses along with the headers of the sites you have visited the authors' names as well as brief information about them. List the sources in a single document for easy access later. Don't forget about those simple tools that can help turn those website links into professional looking bibliographies. Just look up "bibliography generator" or "citation machine."

You can find information quickly by putting in the web browser questions, book titles and author names, serial numbers, model and brand information, specific styles and designs, company websites, and any other useful data.

Reference Materials

Online encyclopedias, e-books and online lectures provide plenty of content to assist you with whatever project you might be working on. So if you wanted to know a popular reference writing guide, a specific book like "The Chicago Manual Style" would come up. This reference is often used by journalists. If I needed to prepare a report on a topic related to a great leader from the 1960s, I could put the individual's name in the search engine browser and then proceed to click on Wikipedia and other similar sites to find out information about that person's life. Simply place the name of what you are looking for in the search engine and then include specific reference materials like "magazines" "ency-clopedias" etc.

Try Different Search Engine Browsers

Place the keywords, subject, phrases, name or other words of what you are looking for in the search engine box. For novices, this box usually appears on the front page of the Internet after you click on the program. For instance, if your homepage is set to "Google" after clicking on your Internet icon, you will see it in plain view. Other popular search engines to date include: Bing, Yahoo! Search, Ask, AOL Search, Wow, WebCrawler and MyWebSearch. The boxes are typically located near the top and toward the center of the pages. Sometimes search engine boxes are at the very top of the screen along a bar with many icons.

Notice keyword suggestions will show up in a dropdown menu, click on one that applies. There are different kinds of searches. Three types of search queries are: Navigational search queries, Informational search queries, and Transactional search queries.

According to an article on Wordstream.com titled, *The 3 Types of Search Queries and How You Should Target Them* by Elisa Gabbert, a navigational search is a query that is for a specific website or webpage. An informational query is a broad search and isn't very direct. Most people will search this way when looking to get a question answered. The transactional search query is a query where the intent is to purchase a product. People who search this way already have the brand name and may include words like: "buy", "purchase" or "order." By now, you probably have done this already. Think of something you might need and perform the search.

Search Results
Sometimes misspellings will throw a search off, so be sure you have spelled the item correctly. Other times, an item might come up in the search engine that has nothing to do with what you are looking for. If this is the case, add specific keywords that describe it such as: color, year, model name, brand, nicknames, etc. Then

press enter so that your search can begin. If you look along the top and sides, you will notice tiny words that mention "ads." These are just what they are and if you don't want to be sold anything, then scroll to sites that provide information.

You can get a feel for what you are looking for by skimming over the descriptions under the titles which are underlined and clickable. Find what you like, simply click on the underlined text. You will then arrive on a page of interest. If it isn't useful, simply go to the top of your screen look to the left and find an arrow that you can click to take you back. It's like flipping a magazine page, you can flip back to the page you were on and continue your search. You can also go back to the site you were visiting by looking to the right of your screen and clicking on a star in one internet browser at the top of the page. Check your favorites or see a tab titled, "history." Click on it and you will see every site you visited.

Special Note: If you want to go forward, checking out other pages, you will see an arrow that points to the right at the top of your screen. If you can't click on it, then you are unable to perform that function.

Specialized Sites

Try searching within the website that has something similar to what you are looking for. Let's say, I want to visit the Target website. This is an American department store. My interest is in jeans for a baby. I would type in www.target.com then I would view the site for a search engine box. I would then put in the size of the jeans, the color and the brand. Right away, I will be taken to a page where I can check out what Target has to offer. But let's say, I don't like their selection, but I think of another department store in my hometown. I would go to a search engine like: www.google.com and then include the name of that store's website since I'm unsure about the spelling of the name. You can check suggestions provided. Then I would scroll down looking for something that says "official site" and then visit the company's webpage I had in mind. Now if I want to take the basic search to the next level, I might add "what are the best sites to purchase baby jeans" or "baby jeans on sale." I could perform a similar search maybe on someone's blog, popular auction site eBay, a local online business that specializes in baby clothes, a social networking site like Twitter, and visit Internet to see if there are related postings. For the budget conscious, you would comparison shop for a specific size, price and possibly color.

Search Better

When the search suggestions that pop up on the drop down menu aren't what you have in mind, you will want to try different search terms. Add more keywords. If you don't want a certain word to come up while you search, you can put a hyphen in front of it. So if you were looking for a street name and you only wanted "Main Avenue Boutique," then include " – Street," so that Main Street Boutique wouldn't come up, this way you are only viewing relevant results.

Maybe you have an exact phrase try putting quotes around it. With so many upgrades to the search engines, this may no longer be necessary, but you can try.

If you want a variety of content such as: videos, images, maps, articles, blogs, audio, and more, then include any one of the words with the keyword or phrase in the search engine box as previously mentioned elsewhere in this book.

Find out what other functions your search engine has to offer. For instance, if you go to the gear icon on Google, you will find that you can conduct advanced searches. This comes in handy if you want to see results from certain domains like .gov sites, read specific languages or find material based on various reading levels.

Sometimes you are not going to find what you are looking for on the first, second, or third try. When this happens you will need to change the wording, but you can also enlist the help of a search engine like ChaCha who has workers who will live chat and assist you with your search. You can also text Google or keyword search "virtual assistant." Popular search commands include:

Quotation marks (")

When you use the quotes surrounding your keyword or phrase they will help you with making your searches more specific.

If you are looking for websites that only have a certain word in them, then you would type in the search engine box the following with whatever it is you are looking for. So let's say I was looking for boys clothes, I would type the following:

inurl:boys clothes

This is what is called an inurl search syntax. It helps you find words within the URL (Uniform Resource Locator.) You may have heard URL mentioned in conversation, this is what some will refer to when typing in an address in the website browser (that's the place where you put in the website address.)

Addition sign (+)

You can use these before the keyword so that the search engine knows that the word must be included. I would also use this sign after a single keyword, followed by another so that the information I am looking for is included in the results.

Subtraction sign (-)

Keeps words out that you don't want. Place the symbol before the keyword.

Asterisks (*)

This mark is usually placed if for instance you have trouble spelling the whole keyword or maybe you have some idea what you are looking for but need some hints. Just place it somewhere after the word.

Meaning of a word

One simple way of looking up a word meaning is to type your word but include the following word in front of it along with the colon, so for instance, it would look like this, define: abash

Google Advanced Short Cuts

If you want to find other ways to make your search easier, check out a long list of advance short cuts. Type in "google advanced shortcuts" and start using some of the tricks provided. You will see short cuts like looking up a book just put the word "book" in front of it. If you are looking up a stock quote, just put "stock" in front of the "company name".

Now there are different search engines for more specific things. Let's say you are only interested in searching for books, then put in "book search engines." Maybe you are only interested in certain topics and what others think about them, put in "blog search engines" or "forum search engines." Sometimes you may only want to view images online; you can do this by putting in "image search engines."

When you are having trouble trying to find something online, there are services available that will help you find what you need. Simply put in the search engine, "need help searching for" and include what is you are looking for.

You will find that if you misspell a word, the search engine will notice it and will ask you, "Did you mean...?" If you misspelled a word, simply click on the correct version.

Some fun things you can do with online research.

1. Begin searching for things related to your age group you didn't know like, "55 years old benefits," "40 year old health changes" or "developmental milestones for five year olds."

2. Check out recent news and views about your ethnicity, culture, faith, etc.

3. Find out what is the latest information related to a current issue you might be facing.

4. Notice articles, blogs and videos on how to perform your job better or some other tasks.

5. List some of the top websites you like based on your preferences. So if you enjoy traveling to Hawaii, you would search for the best websites that provide information on what to do in the state, where to stay, best time to reserve plane tickets, etc.

6. Help someone you know with a research project by asking them about a particular subject matter they need additional information on and then find quotes, statistics, stories, and more about

it.   Be sure to note the website, title of the work, the name of author(s), and the year it was published if necessary.

7. Create a blog or website with your research efforts on a favorite topic. Also, look for sites that might benefit from your work and hopefully will pay you for it.

9 Recreation

In this chapter you will think of things you can do particularly when you are bored. There are a variety of topics mentioned that will help you get started. Take what you already know about the things you do online and just do more with them.

Collecting

What better place than the Internet to learn all about collecting some treasured goods? This is where I discovered how much my collectibles were worth. I also learned who in the neighborhood was buying antiques. Further, I set up a meeting with professional collectors to have my items appraised. You can also have this done online if you know how to take some great photographs and be sure all flaws are in view.

If you are just getting started with collecting, know someone who has an extensive collection of goods, or have been at this for quite some time, then you know searching online is a necessary task to do periodically. You will want to know has the value changed much, are there new items, what websites are selling your items, and more.

Here is a list of things you can do online with your antiques:

1. Take photos and create an online photo album.

2. List items and store in a file on an online storage drive for insurance purposes or prepare for a future sell.

3. Post a valuable on a site that connects sellers with dealers and it doesn't have to be auction sites. Check out other online marketplaces and classifieds.

4.   Type all identifying information about a keepsake in a browser window and just see what comes up.

5.   Find out additional ways to store, organize, and maintain your treasure.

6.   Search for comparable items.

7. Find deals on items so that you can build up your collection.

Comments (Likes and Dislikes), Follows and Shares

Most websites have a section for typing remarks and some will pay money for reviews about their products, services and web pages. This is an important feature on a lot of websites because engaging dialogue creates traffic. Sometimes it can be a bit overwhelming if you are the website or blog owner having to read and filter through the offensive comments and spammers. If you enjoy interacting with a blog or website, then leave feedback. Take notice of comments about a desired product, service or something else on the web page, be sure you are looking at lots of them and visiting other websites as well before you make a purchase.

Likes

You or someone you know may need to accumulate many likes in order to bring awareness about a topic, generate traffic and more. You can do this by paying for likes. You can also pay people to write reviews about your items if you are willing to send them a free sample. People also get likes by commenting on others' pages or encouraging people to "smash the like button."

Dislikes

The thumb down button is quite popular on YouTube. It will only be a matter of time that some of the popular social media outlets will start putting up more variations of good, bad, like, dislike, so-so, alright, okay, fair, etc. expressions. Many lesser known sites already have something similar.

Follows and Shares

If you are interested in following someone then you would act like a fan and receive their updates on Twitter or a similar site. But if you like a posting such as on a blog, website or elsewhere, you would seek the share buttons on the site, select those you have an account with and then post that blog entry or web link to your page; therefore spreading the message that you love or hate the material. If you have a blog or website and would like the share tool to appear on your site, a comment box and other cool things to increase traffic then simply search for them.

Events

Checking for local events and parks is not only easy to do, but most likely you have done this already. However, you can make your search even simpler when you put in the search engine your specific interests rather than just the name of the place you want to visit or a broad search of an occurrence.

Special events in the area might happen during weekdays, weeknights as well as weekends. Adding those words along with interests might bring up desired results. During or near a major holiday include the keyword phrase and what it is you might be looking for. If the event is something advertised on television and you can't remember the specific name just add what you can then include "as seen on TV."

If you are the event planner, there are great instructional videos on preparation. Type into the search engine exactly what your event is and see what comes up. For example, let's say you are planning a family reunion. You might want to check out how others arranged their reunions in your area. You could specifically search for family reunion organizers if you should change your mind about putting one together. You could view sample calendars, agendas, or plans to stimulate ideas. Oftentimes people will upload images of their documents they use to organize events. Switch to Google images, rather than perform the typical search within the browser, to view uploads. Other things you might want to check out include: family reunion letters, templates, clip art, planning forms, activities, themes, and t shirt sayings.

If in doubt about attending a family function or any other event, I created a great resource here for those who tend to get a bit anxious about them *Should I Go to The Party?* by Nicholl McGuire.

Parks

Just when you think you are aware of all the parks and businesses in your community, there is one that you might have overlooked. So if I am conducting a search for a specific amusement park, then I would include the name, but if I don't want to visit that place because I heard it was too crowded and expensive, I could include the park's name and then add the word "alternatives." I would also perform other general searches for keyword phrases such as: "amusement parks" "recreation parks" then include the zip code, city, state or all words to see what else is out there. You can also search "list of parks" "best parks" "popular parks" or type "nearby." If you have permitted the Internet to track your location, you will see what is within close proximity.

Online Fitness

With so many people wanting to lose weight, many businesses are meeting the needs of this ever-popular audience. From shakes to apps to whip people in shape, you can find almost anything online to help you with your personal fitness goals. Start searching for any of the following.

Fitness Trackers

What is keeping you from achieving your fitness goals? Any number of distractions can prevent you from doing what you really want. But you don't have to forget your workout routine anymore; there are apps that can be downloaded to your phone so you can stay motivated. Online fitness websites have trackers that are created to keep people determined to lose weight or stay fit. Visit a site like DailyBurn or similar services by typing "online fitness websites" or "online fitness trackers apps."

Weekly Meal Plans

Discover what you are eating and drinking that is keeping the weight on and what you can ingest that will help you stay healthy. There are many sites that will help you create a weekly meal plan and will also show you meal calories. Keyword search "weekly meal plan" "meal planning ideas" or download and print a personal plan obtained from any site that offers a "weekly meal planner template." Hang this up on your refrigerator and start working on achieving goals! You can also download recipes, grocery list templates, and even arrange to have meals sent to your home. In addition, if you are often pressed for time and can't shop, some grocery stores will allow you to preorder your groceries; clerks will shop for you and have your purchase available for you to pick up.

Search grocery stores in your area to see if they offer these alternative ways of shopping.

Exercise Videos

Do you still wait for an exercise program to watch each day? Do you still purchase exercise videos? Stop! There are so many available online and can also be downloaded. Keyword search "exercise videos" and include that part of your body you would like to work on.

Other things you can check out: online weight loss challenges, fitness consultation, weight loss programs, grocery shopping lists for vegans, juice diets, how to avoid being injured when working out, etc.

Games

For those who simply want to have a little fun online without having to buy a gaming system or portable device, there are plenty of online games. By searching "online games," you will find many different types. But if you don't want to scroll many pages, you might want to search games based on your desired video game genre or learn about other types that might peak your interest. You most likely are familiar with the popular video game genres like: action game, action role-playing, action adventure, fighting game, first-person shooter, multi-player online game, racing video game, shooter game, sports game, beat 'em up, city-building game, and war games. Following are many gaming genres you might want to check out.

1. Affective game
2. Art game
3. Browser game

4. Business simulation game
5. Collectible card game
6. Combat flight simulator
7. Dating sim
8. Dungeon crawl
9. Falling-sand game
10. God game
11. Government simulation game
12. Interactive movie
13. Life simulation game
14. Music video game
15. Nonviolent video game
16. Open world
17. Space flight simulator game
18. Strategy video game
19. Time management
20. Tower base
21. Turn-based strategy
22. Turn-based tactics
23. Vertically scrolling video game
24. Vehicle simulation
25. Visual novel

Most games you don't have to download to your computer. They can be played if your system is already equipped with: Flash, Shockwave, Java or others. You will want to pay attention to ratings when responsible for little ones. Be sure you have age appropriate settings selected before letting children download games to phones and other devices. Also, you will need to set homepages to safe search and use security features to monitor your computers when allowing children to play. You can keyword search "kid friendly search engines" and "children's online safety."

When it comes to purchasing games on or offline, do seek coupon codes and make purchases through links that offer rebates. See the section on coupons in this book.

If you should purchase games on sites known for selling used merchandise, be sure that the seller has been rated highly. Scroll down the list of items he or she has recently sold and notice if there are any games. Sometimes sellers are rated well due to other things they sell, so if there is no extensive history of selling games, do proceed with caution. Also, be sure to check that descriptions are for the game and not just a retail box. Check for any photographs that might reveal what the product looks like before you buy.

Sometimes shipping costs are not included in the price, so before you start typing credit card information, see how much the fees are in advance and where the product is coming from. Some companies will not advertise that their products are being drop-shipped from another country and so the wait time is much longer than if you were to buy from a seller in your state or close by.

Something you will also want to pay close attention to is the company's return policy. Some will not accept any refunds or exchanges and the products are sold as is.

Before you download a game, find out if others have had problems obtaining the game. You might discover that shoppers may have had virus issues, problems with customer service, and more. When it comes to game downloads, you might notice that there are free features and others that are not. If you want to upgrade quickly to receive certain perks in a game, there are usually additional fees involved. Watch for these! Before you know it, your credit card bill is being charged for an upgrade within a game that just might not be worth the money. In addition, before you download check to see if there are any other things that will be showing up on your device. Carefully observe whether you are able to uncheck any additional tools and promotions for other products.

Lastly, check to be sure that your virus and malware software is operable and if you don't have any protection, I strongly advise that you get some. Visit the official site of your Windows operating system and search virus protection then go with what they recommend or search "virus software reviews" in your search engine browser.

Game Play

Sometimes people just don't think about learning how to win at a game. They don't bother to find out what the glitches are and how to successfully win the games before spending hours being frustrated by them. There are plenty of videos online to help solve issues. The Internet can be useful when it comes to gaming strategies, challenges and other useful tips both on and offline. Take a moment to look up your favorite game or someone else's and notice what information comes up about it. Check for upgrades, new characters, cost, style, and even how to make your own game!

Game Creation

Video game programming, online game art and design are ways one can learn more about how to create games. Much software is available for download and online to build up characters, create strategies, and do other fun things to get new games underway. Look up "how to create..." and include what you want to design or "how to..." and add words related to your problem.

Humor

An escape from the daily routines the Internet provides with count-less funny videos, online comic books and strips, crazy photo-graphs, and more you can comment, share, post, or like items. If you are seeking to make your own videos or short films, there are plenty of instructional videos to teach you about lighting, acting, sets, stunts, pranks, and more.

Fun Ideas for Funny Material

Let's say you want to create your own comic book or strip. You could do it the traditional way and sketch out your designs and then print them into book form. However, if you want to take your ideas and drawings to the next level, you can have them show up in pre-drawn characters via an online comic software or video program. You could scan, upload them, and then have them printed in an online book, on a T-shirt, mug, stickers, pens, book bag, etc. You can present your creations as a slideshow too!

A couple of my sons had some funny stories to tell, so I set up a comedy time for them to act a little wild and began recording video. We all laughed much and had a great time looking at the completed videos. As mentioned in this book previously, do check out video editing software. You can create some eye-catching titles, add entertaining effects, and cut out the parts in a video you don't like.

Maybe you want to create a character that looks like you along with including your voice or adding music to something you al-ready started, search for sites that can help. The sky is the limit! I was introduced to different sites that I could use my voice in all sorts of ways from podcasting (similar to radio broadcasting) to rapping.

There are many places online to upload audio. When you have some fun things to say like impersonations, crazy one-liners, and weird sounds, use your audio recording software on your electronic device or those available online to save and share your sounds. Then search for websites in need of your audio. Keyword search: get paid to upload audio or make money uploading files or "share audio websites." Check for places that accept audio sounds used for ring tones, movies, slideshows, etc. People can download these sounds for a fee.

Improve Yourself and Environment

Interested in learning how to do some things better, reach personal goals, or practice what you already know? There are sites that will teach you almost anything. To date, dot coms like: Howcast, HowStuffWorks and Mental Floss can help.

You can also find groups or start your own online for the public or privately with individuals who have common interests. These communities can help you complete life goals, support you when you are having a difficult time, and meet your needs in other ways too. So do search for websites that cater to your needs by searching what your interest is and then include "social groups," "community groups" and "forums."

You can keep up with your success at achieving personal goals by posting your plan and sticking to it on a website of your choice. Search "websites that help with planning goals" or "websites that track goals" or seek apps that can keep you on task.

Ways you can stay motivated to improve your quality of life off-line and online:

1. Download an image or wall paper with an inspiring quote.

2. Listen to thought-provoking audio books online. Many are uploaded to YouTube.

3. Check out social websites where people list good books they have read, personal goals they've met, bucket lists, and more. Join and share some of your thoughts and achievements.

4. Listen to instrumental music online or download meditative music that promotes wellness, eliminates procrastination, helps you study or get a good night rest. Search "brain wave music."

5. Listen to motivational speakers that bring out the best in you. Consider looking up a specific interest along with the word "speakers."

6. Live chat with people who are working toward goals just like you on sites that host videos.

7. Check out blogs that share details on how individuals are overcoming their struggles.

Don't forget to check out the latest environmental groups and activities. You can do this via Twitter. Place the date in the search engine, your city, and include what activity you would like to participate in i.e.) recycle drives, 5k walks, fund-raisers, community clean-up, community block parties, neighborhood watch, town hall meetings, etc. You can also put keywords in the search engine based on your preferences.

Directions, Maps and Geographic Information

It is no longer a challenge to check out a map to get to your destination when you can just point and click on a website and then begin walking down the street online. Google Maps has been one of the best sites for assisting travelers. Take a moment and put in any address you are curious about and you just might be able to see the house or building at that location.

Learn more about geographical information by putting an address in the search engine. You can also type in the word "maps" and include your city or state name to get options.

Some homes and buildings you can only see aerial views due to privacy. If you don't want to be viewed or tracked online, you might want to notify the webmaster of the site you saw your address and images of your home and ask that they remove your information from the listing.

Get printable step-by-step directions by selecting or typing directions along with the business name or residence at the map website.

You can also check out traffic and road conditions via your favorite search engine. Download an app to your portable device to keep you informed of any weather issues, traffic changes, detours, etc. If you are flying in an airplane, you can see how far away you are from your destination, ask the flight attendant for website information or visit the airline's website.

Planning Travel

When planning to travel it doesn't have to be a challenge, but it can be when you are unaware of the many additional features that airlines offer, rental companies advertise and special discounts that hotels give away.

Some things you will want to pay attention to when planning travel include: priority boarding if you check in early, discounts offered through special memberships like AAA, savings and rebates if you book travel through certain websites, coupon codes, and more. You can find out about these things through the main search engines, but you will also want to perform a search within each site.

You can compare prices of 100s of travel sites on one site by using a service like Kayak or Expedia.

For airline savings, search the airline name and then include "promotion code," "flight discounts" or "coupon codes."

To join travel membership clubs, you can search that term but also look up "travel discounts" and don't forget about those services you already have. Find out if they offer membership benefits for travel like warehouse clubs and insurance companies for starters.

TV and Movie

There is so much you can do when it comes to entertaining your-self online via TV and movies. Have you stepped out of the traditional TV and movie watching experience yet? You might want to. Movie trivia, ratings, apps, news, and streaming services are just some of the things people search for.

But what if you wanted to try your hand at acting just for fun? I will tell you that I have personally joined sites locally based that hire extras. If you have a good photo, little or no experience acting, you can connect with some professionals on these sites. They will tell you about local acting workshops and how to obtain other skills to help you get into commercials, documentaries, movies, and more. Check out what TV and movie auditions are happening in your area.

You might not want to be in the movies, but maybe you know someone or a location that could be used for an upcoming film production. You can suggest a person, building or place by contacting film production companies. Lists are available online by state.

Now when it comes to learning more about favorite actors and actresses there are so many sites online. But if you simply want to know about other movies stars have played in the Internet Movie Database is helpful or you can search the actor's name and include the words "movies."

Downloads

Who says you need a television anymore to watch your favorite shows? You can watch television series, documentaries, talk shows, soap operas, comedies, and more online. Shows prior to your birth are available as well on popular video sites and can be downloaded from online bookstores like Amazon Instant Video (amazon.com). Also movies can be watched at Google Play (play.google.com). Users upload old movies from VHS and DVD to YouTube. On that site, you can watch everything for free. But if things should change as this book grows older, you will want to search for new websites "TV show download" "free Internet TV download" "mobile TV download" "TV links download."

Create Your Own TV Channel

Whether you use videos that you already have or look to post new ones, there are websites similar to YouTube that will host your channel. Simply keyword search "how to create my own TV channel" to see what are the latest sites available.

Online Video Making and Software

There are many sites available that can help you with making travel videos, wedding videos, virtual tours, and more with online video makers. You can add music, themes, and effects and instantly make movies. Many computers already have Windows Movie Maker, but there are so many to date that have far more features. You can search "windows movie maker alternatives"

Now if you don't mind having software on your computer, there are some affordably priced programs that have good reviews on Amazon.com. Search within the site to see what is available to date.

Videos

Most people have watched a video on the Internet. But there are many others that do more with videos. Remember those old VHS and DVDs stored away in your home? Well, video matters will incorporate some or all of those home movies into online videos. There are funny snippets from grandparents. Others will use snippets of news, documentaries, block buster movies, and other media for informational purposes in documentaries, commentary, and interviews. However, copyright issues abound so always read disclaimers and know your rights.

Animation is popular on the Internet and users have done some interesting things with cartoons. Some will use the characters on a site like GoAnimate and create entertaining stories. You can find examples on various sites on how to create quality videos on ever-popular YouTube. Feel free to keyword search any of the following ideas to take your video watching and/or making experiences to the next level. Be sure to include keyword phrases like: "How to record" "How to create a video of" "How to make a video about" The more specific you are about what it is you are trying to do, the better the search results.

1. How-to instructional videos

2. Stage performances
3. Video game recording with commentary
4. Reviews or un-boxing of products
5. Artwork showcases
6. Photography videos
7. Motivational speaking
8. Stunts and pranks
9. Events
10. Comedy

Some things people share online include: how to cook certain dishes, how to play instruments, advice on relationships and parenting, how to teach others how to do things like organize things and put together products, find bargains, shop for select products, improve their lives, share personal commentary and news, etc. You will need to have video-making software either on your computer or you can use what is available online as previously mentioned. You can search for the "best video-making software" include the current year.

Slideshows

If you enjoy watching slideshows, you might want to try creating your on slideshows online or offline. Software is available to be downloaded to your computer or you can use products online. Your computer may have come with pre-loaded software so be sure to check first. When searching for software be sure to include "best free online slideshow maker" include the current year if you don't want to purchase anything. (You can do the same for video maker software). However, keep in mind some free software may only be available for trial (which limits some of the features you can use). After using it for a limited time, you might notice a pop up window that will request that you make a purchase.

So what would you be interested in doing when it comes to slideshow creation? Well, have some idea what would look good in a slideshow. Maybe it is you decorated in various costumes, or doing many things like: cooking, cleaning, traveling, etc. You might consider a child's milestones. What about a recent event you attended and all those photos on your phone just waiting to be viewed by others? The ideas are endless.

Keyword search "online slideshow maker" if you want to perform your work online or "slideshow maker downloads" if you don't mind downloading a software program onto your computer. Be sure that you watch for any windows that pop up tempting you to want to download additional software. Be sure to uncheck those boxes.

Once you have a slideshow maker in mind you would like to use, you will notice the many designs you can choose from. Whatever the theme, you would select a template related to the theme. The template is the ready-made design that you will drop those entertaining photographs into. You can get an idea on how others have made slideshows simply by searching "how to make a slideshow."

10 Spirituality

The Internet can be helpful to one who is interested in enhancing one's spiritual relationship with his or her God. With so many people sharing dreams, prophecies, and spiritual experiences online, you will soon discover that you aren't alone. At your fingertips are supportive groups ready to meet whatever your needs might be.

We are human beings made up of mind, body and spirit. So when it comes to matters of the heart, there are many ways to self improve on the Internet. A list of useful things for you to do online is as follows:

1. Seek inspirational music to listen to while you work.

2. Read online bibles based on your belief system.

3. Find a spiritual adviser online who can address your specific needs.

4. Use a personality tool that helps with learning more about you.

5. Search for tools to assist with things like: Christian growth, Christian living, evangelism, counseling, and ethics. You will find books, PDFs, free downloads, slideshows, articles, and more.

6. Check out websites that cater to young believers. You will find toys, books, DVDs, and other helpful products.

7. Type local Christian and include your city/state as well as some things you might be interested in your neighborhood such as: bands, radio, concerts, churches, bookstores, events, dating websites, colleges, etc.

You will find that there are many websites that are unknown. Some have online classes available and offer certificates once completed. You can find out about these by searching "online bible classes certification." Forums, online radio, live chat, live streaming video, and similar places have a myriad of spiritual topics. There are also blogs, social networking pages, and directories created by people from many different denominations to encourage one another. Consider joining some groups.

Some things I have found helpful when it comes to biblical study are: online bibles like "bible gateway" and "bible hub", online bible concordance, bible dictionary, bible quotes, and even states that are along the "bible belt." Find biblical names too and the stories associated with them. If you can recall portions of Scripture, the rest will show up when you type them in the search engine.

I have personally found my spiritual life improved immensely in so many ways because I prayed and was guided by my God to the needed material at the right place and at the right time. God isn't just in the church, He is online too!

Counseling/Therapy

When it comes to those issues that bother you within, the Internet is one of the best resources to look up any condition! You can even chat live with some counselors, researchers and others knowledgeable about your issue. From spiritual to mental, you will be able to connect the dots about your situation without having to spend thousands paying someone to aid you. Start with a simple topic of your choosing, then research ways to cope or manage whatever ails you. There are usually organizations online that deal with many conditions and some of them offer free or discounted service offline. Be sure to check websites that offer local coupons for therapy. Consider subscribing to a professional's list, obtain free information, and send correspondence about your problem.

11 Dating

If you are married or in a committed relationship, you can skip this section, that is unless you are helping a friend, then keep reading. The online world of dating is so easy to enter into that one can become addicted with the rush of emotions that come with meeting someone new. This can be a good thing when you settle down with the right person or a bad thing if you are in a steady relationship, but still looking, or you often meet Mr. or Ms. Wrong online. Whatever your situation, you have to know when to take those long needed breaks from the Internet and get back to appreciating the life you have offline.

Online Dating

Many singles often find meeting people offline a bit of a challenge and prefer to make a connection online, and then later meet in person. For those interested in dating, there are plenty of websites available. In addition, numerous resources are available on these sites to help singles with dating. On the web, you will find many interest specific dating websites. For instance, if you would like to date a millionaire, there are many sites that cater to those who seek to date wealthy and attractive men and women. Maybe you prefer dating people within a certain age group; there are sites that are specifically designed for seniors, twenty, thirty and forty something's.

Daters have a certain gender, ethnicity, religion, location, height, body build, fetish, and other preferences. There are dating sites that will help make your connections for you. So if you desired a man or woman who is tall, fit, from the United States, has a pet, no children, about 20 plus, and lives in Texas, then there would be a computer generated match for you! To learn more about what is available to you online, simply type "dating websites" in your browser then include a few of your interests. For example a keyword specific phrase might be, "free heterosexual dating websites in Ohio."

Advice

When it comes to dating issues, there are countless reports advising people on how to solve their problems. Depending on what your relationship concern, you can have the advice delivered in a number of ways. If you conduct your search including the phrase and keywords like: video, podcast, book, tweet, slide-shows, or a specific name of a website, you will receive information from a myriad of resources rather than taking whatever comes up in the search engine. Forums are another way people obtain relation-ship advice.

Dating Website Reviews

Many daters will check review sites before joining a dating web-site. Most of them will list 10 of the best dating sites. They will sometimes include a rating, the type of relationships, cost, gender ratio, etc. According to ConsumerSearch.com, Dating Site Re-views, they conducted research and found negative reviews. Users complained of "dishonest profiles, demanding people and scammers. Some also complained about the dating sites inflating subscriber numbers, making people who sign up think they'll have plenty of choices, when most of the users are actually inactive. One constant complaint was about automatic billing and another was about suggested potential mates who are either nonpaying members or no longer visit the site.

Dating Apps

With so many dating apps popping up everyday, you might want to research which one is right for you based on whatever device you will be accessing the websites. For instance, you might look up "dating apps iPhones" or "top dating apps + include the current year". You can research dating apps based on what you are interested in as well. For instance, if a woman is older and seeking a younger man, she could look up "cougar dating app."

Matchmaking Services

There are plenty of matchmaking sites, but it would make sense to check reviews first before joining. You can keyword search a specific name or add some preferences to the keywords "match-making services" such as the city and state. People who don't want to be bothered with browsing dating profiles and running the risk of being scammed and are short on time, register with these professional services.

Online and Virtual Dating

If you are looking for a fun and safe way to date, there is online virtual dating. When searching for sites, you will find that these websites have cartoon like images that are used to help you make an online connection. You can create your own avatars, explore cool venues with them, communicate through chat, and do other interesting things without ever having to meet your connections offline. For teens there are dating simulation games where they too can connect with virtual dates.

Speed Dating

A speedy way people connect with other people offline is through various speed dating events. You can research those by including the keyword, your preference (professional, casual, heterosexual, etc.) and your location to find out more about up-coming functions. Speed dating is a fun way to meet many singles in one night. Participants are seated across from one another talking for a limited time with a card that they use to rate whether they made a match. Then on to the next date once the host rings a bell. The time frame is about five minutes or longer depending on the speed date event.

Special Preferences (compatibility questionnaires)

Sometimes one is simply not ready to brave all that is out there when it comes to dating. If so, you might want to take personality tests to learn more about yourself. If you should decide to register with a few dating websites, check to see they have questionnaires for you to fill out. This helps their system find suitable matches for you. They can be quite long and tedious to fill out, but they are worth it. Look up dating websites with compatibility question-naires.

12 Did You Know?

You can have an abundance of knowledge using the Internet; yet a user will never be able to fully comprehend or master everything there is to know about it. New websites are built within minutes and the competition can be fierce when it comes to driving traffic to one's creations. How you find out what is out there that can better assist you with your personal and professional goals can be done in many different ways. You can begin your quest of the latest websites, trends, and more by searching for them. Specific searches will help you connect with the right websites. Remember include the current year, the television show, book or magazine you might have saw the new item, add words like "new," "latest" or "current" to your keyword phrase.

Did you know there are a host of timeless tools that won't be going anywhere anytime too soon specifically designed to help you track, sort, develop, arrange, influence, prioritize, process, listen, learn, counsel and more. Now how might you discover those top websites that will help you with administration and management on the job or others that assist with communications and creativity? What about the best sites that might elevate your commission from sales and teach you more about persuading others? You might have some personal challenges with organizing, motivating others, sticking to tasks, meeting goals, and more. So what kind of helpful Internet related inventions could you be missing out on? Well in order to solve that problem, I would take the time to note what is the most important thing I need to find before I begin my Internet session? You have to become your own instructor teaching yourself to be disciplined to the task while staying sharp in your field of study.

Most people don't think beyond the classroom or workplace when using the Internet, and so the knowledge they have obtained becomes outdated because they never bother to utilize the professional vocabulary they know to find out what new products and services are out on the web.

Try This Exercise

Have a notepad and pen ready and start listing some of those words you use in your industry. The key is to get the most out of your Internet experiences that will aid you in your career, with your family, and to problem solve in other areas of your life. When you use the knowledge you have acquired, you will soon discover what creations key developers in your industry have built. You will also find out things you never knew from something as small as how to organize a thing to what to do after a loved one has passed away. The Internet is like a rabbit hole, once one starts digging you never know where that hole might take you.

Maybe there is something you always wanted to do or become a master at it. Remember, in order to get good at whatever that might be, you have to spend some time daily learning about it. Give yourself at least 40 minutes each day discovering new information, reading about it and then putting what you know into practice. So let's say your goal is to lose weight. It would make sense to begin searching for information related to your goal. Therefore, note what you want to know and don't leave your computer until you have some sort of strategy you are willing to follow. So your plan might look like this.

1. Things I am doing wrong and health issues I currently have.

2. My meal plan including times I will eat and how much.
3. Exercises I will do daily.
4. Supplements I need to take.
5. Dietician and appointment to meet.

All of the information you need for each point would be found on the Internet. The key is to implement what you know long after the computer gets shut off. So the time you set aside for research, eating, exercise, and more would be noted and each day you would remind yourself to stick to the plan. You create reminders and post those on places like the mirror in your bathroom, the refrigerator or near an exit of your home.

The following are some categories you might be interested in obtaining further knowledge. Notice the kind of keywords I included to perform searches. With each one you can add, delete or rearrange words. Consider keywords like "top 10" "best" "popular" and remember to add the current year if need be. Conduct these searches on Google but also consider re-wording and doing the same on social media, forums and article directories.

Technical Related Things
What new software for...
How to analyze....
What websites educate on...
How do I compile...
What inventions have been created to...
How has XYZ been modified compared to...

Office Support
How do I manage...
What tools to use to make...

How to improve...
How to organize...
How to balance...
How to budget...
What things needed to coordinate...
How to plan for...

Teaching
How to coach...
Goal setting for...
How to influence...
What tools needed to collaborate...
How to effectively communicate
What new programs have revolutionized...
How to train...
What education is needed for...

Researching and Analyzing
How to administer...
The amplified version of...
How to audit...
How to detect...
How to apply
Samples of...
How to compose...
How to construct...
How to conduct...
How to assess...
Investigations on...
Discoveries made...

Forecasts of...

Think of other things you may want to know more about when it comes to helping and providing care-giving services, managing finances, and other skills.

Helping Others

How to facilitate...

How to foster...

How to guide...

How to mentor...

Services to optimize...

Tips on nurturing...

How to encourage...

Finances

How to appraise...

How to adjust...

How to calculate...

Tips on increasing...

How to save...

Where to shop....

How to reduce...

Where to invest...

How to fund...

Consumer reports on...

Other Keywords You Can Use for Various Skills

accomplishments of...

achievements made in...

Who conceptualized...?

contributors of...

demonstrations of...

remodeled...

proposals of...

solved problems with...

winners of...

How to integrate...

advice on...

founded...

How to perform...

ways to promote

advice on reshaping...

How to repair...

The following is a quick list of some utilities you can start looking up now and start using on your computer or portable devices. You can find all of these tools within your search engines, the best is Google.

- Desktop customization tools
- Web tool for organizing research, music, meeting, projects...
- Fix (include your favorite browser) and Internet connections
- Downloading videos and songs from Internet
- Image snipping
- Uploading images and video to social networking pages and blogs
- Help with studying
- Time management
- Writing books, screenplays, poems...
- Lose weight
- Digital tools to help with online snooping

- Convert measurements
- Convert currencies
- Calculate anything
- Get definitions
- Get the time
- Internet marketing
- Searching Internet
- Sports scores and schedules
- Sunrise and sunset times
- Track packages
- Earthquake activity
- Real-time stock quotes

When looking up these tasks, to find out the latest tool available, you will use the keyword related to your interest or industry and then include the current year. For example, "screen recording software 2020 for market research"

Still More to Do on the Internet

When there is free time during the day or things have slowed down, I have learned valuable things from during random searches on the Internet. After finding out something useful, I would feel like "If only I would have done this a month ago..." Here are some things you can do that might be beneficial to you and your family.

1. Search for remedies related to a chronic health ailment related to you or a member of your family.

2. Find out side effects of certain prescription medicines.

3. Learn more about your job title or someone else's.

4. Find out more ways to use the items that you already have such as: computer equipment, mobile devices, appliances, garden gadgets, hair tools, cooking items, etc.

5. Seek out fun things to do with children based on age group.

6. Coupon search for your favorite items then print out and take to the store.

7. Compare prices of some things needed for self, home or work.

8. Sign up for a free online class and begin lessons the same day.

9. Watch feel-good music videos and documentaries when you don't feel like yourself.

10. Look for ways to fix broken items. Type what it is that is broken and how to fix.

11. List items for sell you no longer need or use. Find out "websites to sell stuff."

12. Surf the classifieds for products you need. Keyword search: top classifieds and add your city and state.

13. Check for local events and announcements, and then mark your calendar.

14. Find old friends via a social networking site. Keyword search: "top social networking sites."

15. Visit alternative sites to the ones you typically visit, so instead of spending time on Yahoo, check out other search engines. Do the same with other Internet routines.

16. Start a new website, blog, submit an article, leave comments, write reviews, etc.

17. Go to church online. Type your denomination and then include "online churches."

18. Find new ways to arrange furniture in your dwelling.

19. You can discover random sites by joining a website that will help generate some based on the interests you put in your profile. For many years StumbleUpon has helped their users

discover cool sites. You can check for StumbleUpon alternatives or sites like StumbleUpon to find more.

20. Try new software i.e.) learning a foreign language, drawing, organizing, photo editing, etc.

21. Check out real time webcams and traffic cams from around the world.

22. Learn about interesting things simply by typing anything in the search engine you always wanted to know about. Be careful with this suggestion, you might want to set a timer.

23. View cool artwork, shop or discover new websites for inspiration.

24. Select a new audio player that you can choose any music. Keyword search: audio players.

25. Listen to a podcast or talk radio. There are plenty so keyword search what you want to listen to and then include "podcast" or "talk radio" add other useful words.

26. Learn more about your favorite musicians. You can find out every song they have recorded, where they are from, what they did before becoming a superstar, etc.

27. Look for sites that offer giveaways, freebies. Keyword search: free...then include what you would like for free. You can also check for free movies, music, credit report...just be sure the sites you visit sincerely offer free things.

28. Check out locations that help you get in shape or stay fit. Keyword search: top 10 fitness websites.

29. View the latest websites that offer news about a variety of subjects including conspiracy theories.

30. Search for popular websites based on your preferences i.e.) popular hairstyling websites.

31. Participate in best baby photo contests, writing contests, gaming competitions, online sweepstakes, etc.

32. Check out virtual equipment i.e.) online music mixers--instruments, sing a-longs, keyboards, Virtual DJ (disc jockey) turntables, etc.

33. Search your name and others that you know include social networking websites, affiliations, and more.

34. Learn about body language. Keyword search: body language interpretation.

35. Track progress of stocks before investing. You can make a game of it. Keyword search: virtual stock market game.

36. Look up the origin of holidays. You will find fascinating information you did not know.

37. How to organize a drawer, closet, cabinet, holiday decor, papers, etc.

38. Where to find cheap (you fill in the blank).

39. Where to go in (include your city) in the (include the current season).

40. Places to donate (include what you would like to give away).

41. Send emails to companies you do business explaining why you like or dislike their product or service. Offer some suggestions.

42. Visit not-so popular sites to shop for things like: tools, toys, clothes, home items, etc.

43. Search for things you or someone else you know can do offline when bored.

44. Learn how to do something you already know how to do better from folding clothes to conversing before a live audience.

45. Find lost relatives.

46. Discover which countries or cites are the best places to visit or live.

47. Search for best communities in your area for things like: schools, low property taxes, shopping, jobs, etc.

48. Find new crafts to build or repurpose old items.

49. Take virtual tours of famous buildings, cities and other historical stuff.

50. Visit the neighborhoods of distant relatives virtually. You can do this by obtaining their street information and then going online to view via Google maps.

51. Collect useful news clippings and organize according to your interest on a social bookmarking site or save under a favorites folder.

52. Create poetry online and submit your work to sites in need of poets.

53. Window shop or watch old commercials online of items you grew up with when you were a child.

54. Check out old stamps, coins, and other collectibles to see how much they are currently worth.

55. Look up sites that are in need of whatever you can provide others. So if your hobby is building model cars, painting scenery or doing hair then you would look for websites in need of images or your skills.

56. Seek out new friends.

57. Send direct messages to some of the people in your social networks.

58. Research additional ways to use practical items from paper clips to plastic containers.

59. Find out how to construct something in your residence that the whole family can benefit from.

60. Note cool websites that are entertaining, smart, save you time, money or fun.

61. Take the time to fill out your profiles on websites you joined.

62. Create an infographic (it looks like an online wall poster with statistical data, charts, maps, etc.) of something you feel passionate about or take a look at what your resume might look like as a visual. You can promote it on sites that display infographics.

63. Seek out ways to repurpose material you have already created online.

64. Reach out to other bloggers and ask them to write a review or feature your product on their pages.

65. List all the things you like to use then look for websites that showcase testimonials. Contact website owners.

66. Search for the latest apps for your computer operating system.

67. Check for new add-ons or extensions of the Internet program that you use.

68. Consider researching apps by specific needs in the App store and other places where apps are sold. For instance, what trending apps are available to help you with things like: dating in your local area, cooking simple meals, tracking fitness goals, home organization, office tasks, shopping for specific goods, saving money, and more.

69. Find things on the web that relate to a problem someone else is trying to solve, but the person doesn't have the time or patience to look up an issue.

70. Find people who have started meet up groups and special events in your area based on favorite hobbies.

Can you think of more things to do on the Internet?

Be Inspired to Do Something Different

Now that you have been encouraged to step out the box and do even more remarkable things on the Internet, take some of those ideas that jumped out at you on the previous list, write them down on slips of paper, then fold them up, stick them in a jar, tray, or dish near your computer, and when you are bored, just pick from them.

The key when using the Internet is to do things like: periodically break dull routines, get more out of your sessions, and hopefully make your life a bit more interesting offline too. Consider that many of the websites that you have been loyal to over the years will eventually change and so will you. Some companies will alert their users that they are making changes while others not so much. Sometimes these so called improvements actually cause more problems for loyalists, because they have been accustomed to doing the same things on the websites and so when change comes they aren't ready and don't want it.

Policy changes, privacy infringements, suspensions over things that were never issues before, fees, complicated features, slow servers, and other things can make anyone stop using a site or worse take a long break from visiting, shopping or registering with websites. Other times it isn't that sites have changed, but your thought processes, interests and more when approaching the Internet have because you are simply bored on and offline. People who become too idle tend to do reckless things on the Internet from bullying to hacking websites.

When you notice that you are weary of some sites and others are just not functioning as good as they once did, consider looking for alternatives like this guide has repeatedly suggested. I have been known to delete my accounts from old sites, search for alternatives and register with the new ones. By making some personal changes, I have had better Internet experiences and even asked myself sometimes, "Why didn't I do these things a long time ago? Why did I stick with this website for so long?"

There have been times that I have taken down items over the years as a publisher and went back to being just a user. Then found other useful sites and became active on them. I have had some negative things occur online from competitors flagging me on popular sites to sensitive people leaving negative comments about articles and videos I have posted. But my experiences haven't been so disheartening that I would ever want to stop using the Internet even when scammers turned me off. Instead, I looked forward to the good times connecting with people, discovering new sites, and learning new things. I have had many good times on the Internet, too numerous to count. From strangers sharing how they have been helped by my uploaded materials (books, articles, audio, etc.) to customers leaving positive ratings about business transactions we have had. So I am grateful and humble to be a part of the Internet community.

Some people are content with using the Internet for basic tasks while others want to create things that will make a lasting impact. Whatever the reasons we use it, no one can dispute how valuable it is to our lives. I must add the web is indeed one of the best inventions by far in our modern society. I look forward to a future where we can use other senses to communicate with others online while getting needs met far beyond our imaginations. I can't tell you how impressed I was years ago when I saw that one could check on his or her residence via the Internet or connect a doll to the computer while she is left to entertain children. I was impressed with buying food via websites until one company I ordered from mailed some stale edibles to one of my relatives. Even though this happens offline too, I prefer to walk or ride down the street to take my item back then to go to a post office, wait in line to return the package (or have someone on the receiving end do it) and then wait for the company to get the item and then wait again for them to process my refund (by the way this has taken as long as a month for me). Meanwhile, I hoped the whole time everything was completed within the company's limited time for accepting returns. I think that this is why offline stores will never go out of style, because some things you just don't want to have to wait weeks for and you definitely don't want to have to pay ridiculous expedited shipping costs either if you don't have to.

There are many inventions that have been created to connect with us on an emotional, physical and spiritual level. Do take some time out to see what the newest products are. You may be missing out on something that could very well make your life easier. Keyword search: "new Internet inventions" or use a keyword phrase for your specific need. Maybe you would like to find out what inventions have been created to help with opening something, building a desired product, shopping for clothing, assisting with a problem, or designing an item for one of your rooms. Make time everyday to explore the Internet to see what it has to offer.

To date, there are websites that help with your online clothing shopping. They do require webcams. On these sites a shopper can stand before his or her screen and allow the device to display his or her body type (clothed of course) to see how he or she looks in clothing and accessories online. Further, using a photo or taking a video in real time can help you see what make up looks good on you, what hairstyles are a good match, what color is right for you, and what are some other cool things to do online? So find out what fun stuff you can do by taking the time to research. Periodically seek out "fun stuff using..." then include what it is you are curious about.

Change can be good when it comes to Internet usage if you know what you want, what you won't tolerate online, and what sites will provide the best benefits to you and your family. Break some dead routines today, incorporate some new ones, and keep on surfing that 'Net! Thanks for reading this guide!

Books and Blogs by Author

What Else Can I Do on the Internet? (eBook version)
Too Much, Too Soon Internet Dating Blues
Black Friday, Cyber Monday Strategies to Use Year Round
Should I Go to the Party?
She's Crazy
Genealogy X: What to Expect When Researching Family History
Socially Sweet, Privately Cruel Abusive Men
Say Goodbye to Dad
Tell Me Mother You're Sorry
Know Your Enemy: The Christian's Critic
When Mothers Cry
Laboring to Love an Abusive Mate
Laboring to Love Myself
Floral Beauty on a Dead End Street
Spiritual Poems by Nicholl

Blogs by Nicholl McGuire Media

ThingstoDoBored.blogspot.com
ApartmentLeasingTips.blogspot.com
WorkPlaceProblems.blogspot.com

Connect with the Author

nichollmcguire@gmail.com
YouTube channel: nmenterprise7
Twitter @nichollmcguire
Pinterest Nicholl McGuire
Subscribe to my blog: nichollmcguire.blogspot.com
Virtual Assistance: nichollmcguiremedia.blogspot.com